Social Reproduction Theory
and the Socialist Horizon

Mapping Social Reproduction Theory

Series editors Tithi Bhattacharya, Professor of South Asian History and the Director of Global Studies at Purdue University; and Susan Ferguson, Associate Professor, Faculty of Liberal Arts, Wilfrid Laurier University

Capitalism is a system of exploitation and oppression. This series uses the insights of Social Reproduction Theory to deepen our understanding of the intimacy of that relationship, and the contradictions within it, past and present. The books include empirical investigations of the ways in which social oppressions of race, sexuality, ability, gender and more inhabit, shape and are shaped by the processes of creating labour power for capital. The books engage a critical exploration of Social Reproduction, enjoining debates about the theoretical and political tools required to challenge capitalism today.

Also available

Disasters and Social Reproduction:
Crisis Response between the State and Community
Peer Illner

Social Reproduction Theory:
Remapping Class, Recentering Oppression
Edited by Tithi Bhattacharya

Women and Work:
Feminism, Labour, and Social Reproduction
Susan Ferguson

Social Reproduction Theory and the Socialist Horizon

Work, Power and Political Strategy

Aaron Jaffe

Foreword by Cinzia Arruzza

PLUTO PRESS

First published 2020 by Pluto Press
345 Archway Road, London N6 5AA

www.plutobooks.com

Copyright © Aaron Jaffe 2020

The right of Aaron Jaffe to be identified as the author of this work has been
asserted in accordance with the Copyright, Designs and Patents Act 1988.

British Library Cataloguing in Publication Data
A catalogue record for this book is available from the British Library

ISBN   978 0 7453 4053 1   Hardback
ISBN   978 0 7453 4054 8   Paperback
ISBN   978 1 7868 0635 2   PDF eBook
ISBN   978 1 7868 0637 6   Kindle eBook
ISBN   978 1 7868 0636 9   EPUB eBook

This book is printed on paper suitable for recycling and made from fully
managed and sustained forest sources. Logging, pulping and manufacturing
processes are expected to conform to the environmental standards of the
country of origin.

Typeset by Stanford DTP Services, Northampton, England

Simultaneously printed in the United Kingdom and United States of America

Contents

Acknowledgments

Acknowledgments are tricky. Social reproduction theory points me towards a dense web of social relations that made the developments I am offering here possible. Indeed, our intellectual and political communities are at least as responsible as the individuals who, through them, have the chance to develop and then share their theoretical reflections. So, I see what I have written here as part of an extended and iterative practice - one through which communities of struggle, and the theoretical attempts at self-clarification that stem from them, can create radicalizing dynamics.

So, first and foremost, I thank the militants who have already, are now, and who will continue to be committed to revolutionary socialist struggle. Wherever and whenever this book finds you, I thank you. I want to acknowledge not so much a debt, but a radical and enriching gift. I deeply hope some of what you find in here will be helpful as well.

I thank Cinzia Arruzza, Jules Gleeson, Kate Doyle Griffiths, Michelle O'Brien, and Joshua Pineda, each of whom have been generous with their unique gifts of insight, and in their unwavering support for collective, militant commitments. Cinzia opened the door to social reproduction theory for me with her framing metaphor of a 'beating heart' of capital, and was my first point of contact with International Women's Day strikes. Jules organized Leftovers forums both online and live at conferences which, in addition to providing the most trenchant left-analyses of gender available, helped me workshop early drafts of chapters. More than anyone else, Kate created a political home for me in Red Bloom, and developed the notion of 'crisis' and specific account of 'value' that I rely on here. Michelle provided the conceptual key to thinking the gendered division of labor, taught me much about logistics organizing, and kept me focused over countless hours of co-working sessions. Joshua helped form my thinking about the limits of radical theory, its connection to practice, and invited me to radical reading, gaming, and dining groups when I really needed these social connections. I have relied on each of your intellects and politics on every page of this book – in some cases from long before I knew I would be writing it, and in others with the crystal-clear formulations that I did not know I was reaching for until you handed them to me.

Much of the early work for the book was done in Montreal in the pre-pandemic summer of 2019. I am immensely grateful for the large table and excellent drinks at Café Replika, the public facilities of the BAnQ Grande Bibliothèque, and the office space and library resources provided by William Clare Roberts at McGill University. I should also acknowledge the material support for research and travel provided by the Liberal Arts department at The Juilliard School.

Thank you Tithi Bhattacharya, Sue Ferguson, and David Shulman for your confidence in my ability to write this book, and for your feedback and continuous support throughout the process. The anonymous reviewers, Jules, Josh, Cinzia, Lee Cyphers, Ruby Kinney, and Rohan Quinby sharpened the ideas and their expression with their sensitive eyes at various stages of preparation, as did Elaine Ross with Pluto Press, at the copy-editing phase.

Finally, a deep thank you from the heart to Emmanuelle Sirois. I have learned so much from you about being a feminist in both theory and practice. Your love, support, confidence, and patience throughout my writing has been a godsend.

Foreword

Cinzia Arruzza

Toward the end of March 2020, Texas Lieutenant Governor Dan Patrick made headline news by arguing on Fox News that he and other American grandparents would be willing to take a chance and sacrifice themselves for the sake of saving the economy for their children and grandchildren. While meant to package opposition to COVID-19 lockdown measures in heroic, even patriotic, garments, this comment was widely—and correctly—interpreted as what it actually was: a utilitarian economic calculus about the expendability of human lives, or in more prosaic terms, a further demonstration that the Republican Party and Trump's administration had gone morbid.

At the time I am writing this text, the United States is by far the world's leading country in terms of number of COVID-19 infections (an average of 45,000 new cases a day, for a total of 5.4 million). The death tally, more than 170,000 deaths recorded by the *New York Times*, a number that admittedly underestimates the actual death tally, makes Patrick's comments sound even more ominous. It is not by chance that the three nations faring the worst in terms of management of the pandemic are the United States, Brazil (where the death tally is already at more than 100,000 and the pandemic is disproportionately affecting indigenous people), and India: three countries governed by an authoritarian neo-liberal far right.

The COVID-19 pandemic, which has already caused almost one million deaths worldwide, has made more visible our common social and economic interdependence at both national and transnational level. We are not social monads, but rather social beings who are deeply bound together throughout and between countries. The pandemic has also made more transparent the central contradiction between profit-making and life-making characterizing the distinctly capitalist organization of social reproduction. This contradiction has become apparent not only in the right-wing opposition to lockdown measures in the name of keeping "the economy" going.

Insofar as the pandemic has disrupted capitalist normality, transnational value and distribution chains, and patterns and pace of production, it has also brought to light the centrality of social reproductive activities, many of which labeled as "essential work" during the pandemic crisis. The lives of workers engaged in social reproduction were, and remain continuously devalued. The workers who proved to be the indispensable building blocks of our societies, on whose work we all depend for the reproduction of our lives, are the very same people whose often gendered and racialized lives are being treated as dispensable. Work from home with closed schools and no childcare or elderly care provisions in place, has taken an enormous mental and physical toll especially on women. The deep financial crisis of the higher education sector in the United States, which has pushed many campuses to, hopefully briefly, reopen even in the absence of basic containment and tracking measures, is also making apparent the irrationality and fragility of the private, neoliberal organization of education.

Within this context of suspended capitalist normality, two irreconcilable worldviews and collective and individual practices have come to the forefront. These can be best appraised by referring to two opposed instances of social and political mobilization that have characterized the first six months of pandemic crisis in the United States. On the one hand, far-right, libertarian and white supremacist anti-lockdown protests, often politically orchestrated and small in number, have manifested a straightforward refusal of any kind of social responsibility and solidarity, accused nurses of being agents of infection, dismissed the risks for people's health and lives by either relying on conspiracy theories or by openly endorsing ableism and social Darwinism for the sake of "liberty" and of the "economy."

On the other hand, the explosion of what can be easily considered as one of the greatest social uprisings in the history of the United States, prompted by the brutal assassination of George Floyd in May 2020 by the police and during which millions of people have willingly faced the risk of contagion by taking to the streets to fight institutionalized racism and defend the right of Black and Brown people to breath: a right denied both by the racialized differential impact of the pandemic and by the police's systemic racism.

On the one hand, "liberty fighters" refusing to wear masks and literally spitting in the face of other people who tried to confront them, on the other hand the emergence and proliferation of forms and groups of mutual aid and social reproduction from below: from the distribution of masks, hand-sanitizers, and snacks during the protests, to the organization of mutual aid to cater to the basic needs of people at high risk of death by COVID-19 in towns and neighborhoods.

These two instances speak of two opposed forms of response to the disruption of the "normal" capitalist organization of production and social reproduction: the first, by opposing social distancing of any kind, paradoxically exacerbated individualism and social isolation as a response to the new transparency of our common social interdependence; the second put in place solidarity and alternative forms of social reproduction to support those left behind by the crisis. Both the strength of solidarity and the organization of alternative forms of social reproduction grew along with collective resistance and struggle.

What emerged in this confrontation was not just the opposition between irreconcilable political projects: the divergence in politics, individual behaviors and collective practices also reflected a fundamental difference in implicit or explicit ethical commitments, as people had to ask themselves and provide responses to questions concerning, for example, what lives have value and the meaning of social responsibility. This social and political context makes Aaron Jaffe's book both timely and urgent.

In this highly original book, Jaffe provides social reproduction theory with a sustained discussion of its ethical stakes and implicit assumptions. This discussion turns around the development of what Jaffe calls a socio-historical philosophical anthropology, one able to offer a critical alternative to the anthropological atomism and individualism that is the fundamental philosophical assumption behind much of the liberal tradition.

Jaffe's philosophical anthropology is based on the careful unpacking of the notion of "labor power," which is central to social reproduction theory, focusing especially on the meaning of "power," understood as both capacity and potentiality. From this viewpoint, Jaffe's book is an excellent complement to the previous instalment of the Mapping Social Reproduction Theory series: Susan Ferguson's *Women and Work* (2019), which focused on feminist conceptualizations of women's work and on the meaning of "labor" in the concept of labor power.

Jaffe's book operates on the assumption that social theory is always grounded in ontological or philosophical anthropological views, which may or may not be made explicit within the theory itself. And moreover, that such a grounding is even more unavoidable in the case of critical social theory, as critique always implicitly entails some ethical, evaluative or normative standards of one kind or another. And so, if social reproduction theory is a *critical* theory, its critique of capitalism must in some way be grounded in views about what kind of beings we are and what is conducive to a good life (or better, to "good lives" in the plural).

These views need not be ahistorical or ontological in a robust sense, need not be based on transhistorical and dubious notions of "human nature," and certainly need not to abstract from relevant differences among human beings and their specific social, historical, and cultural contexts. And in fact, Jaffe crucially insists that the philosophical anthropology he proposes is a socio-historical one: we are the kind of beings we have become through our social and historical practices. Within this framework, Jaffe's book addresses two key questions: first, why capitalism harms our living personality, hence what are the grounds of our anti-capitalist critique; and second, what is conducive to the flourishing of our individual powers and to the realization of our potentialities in such a way that others' living personalities are also enhanced, based on the recognition that we are socially interdependent beings and not social monads.

Using this approach, Jaffe is able to develop a notion of "powers" that can ground critiques of ableism and social Darwinism through an examination of the specific harm caused by the racism, ableism, transphobia, and misogyny ingrained in the capitalist organization of social reproduction. For example, Jaffe's take on disability is that the very notion of disability emerges from a social and historical process of evaluation of which "powers" to labor or which living capacities are worth being bought or even developed in the first place, processes heavily informed and constrained by capitalist needs.

Jaffe's book is ultimately a book about freedom. Jaffe is, in this sense, a very careful reader of Marx, for—contrary to widespread mistaken assumptions—Marx's central concern and guiding problem throughout his life and work was, indeed, freedom, rather than equality. The pandemic, moreover, has made more visible the necessity of developing a simultaneously social and individual notion of freedom, based on the recognition of the social relations that bound us together.

Social reproduction theory is well situated for reviving and continuing this line of thought in Marx, for it allows us to articulate a critique not merely of patterns of redistribution and inequality, but of an entire social form of life-making that makes genuine freedom impossible. It also allows us to develop a non-economic reductionist view of class as a central agent for the struggle for freedom, a view that – as Jaffe stresses – takes forms of lived experience inflected and constrained by various kinds of oppression to be *constitutive* features of what counts as class, rather than external add-ons to an abstract and economist notion of class.

While these insights are often implicit in social reproduction analyses and elaborations, Jaffe makes them explicit by articulating a philosophical theory capable of explaining why the forms of life capitalism develops are exploitative, alienating and oppressive. Accordingly, Jaffe also reframes what he calls the socialist horizon as a horizon of freedom: "Invoking the socialist horizon of emancipation means developing and fighting for the freedom of our lived, embodied personalities. It is the emancipation of our labor powers from the needless experience of their constraint … The goal is genuine freedom for living personalities. That means the emancipation of each person's living personality and need-satisfying capacities" (p. 97).

The pandemic has brought to the forefront the ethical and evaluative dimension of political struggle, making more apparent what the existential stakes of the struggle are. Jaffe's original contribution to social reproduction theory offers us important theoretical and philosophical tools to make us able to wage this struggle, and possibly win.

Introduction:
Why Theorize Social Reproduction?

The role of women, it's funny you said that because I've always viewed myself as a teacher, and I remember when through this process … there have been so many interviews with different people and I remember one of the interviews someone sent me, and they had put at the bottom of the screen "activist". And I laughed, I was sitting with one, you know, one my best friends and I said, "activist?", and she was dead serious and she looked at me and she said, "you are," and I said, "I am! You're right, yes, I am not just a teacher, I'm an activist!" And so, a lot of women have really led this movement … We learned that you don't have to have a title, you don't have to have a position, you just have to have courage and a backbone to stand up for yourself, your state, and your kids, and that's what we did! (Katie Endicott, on the West Virginia public school employees' strike)[1]

Social Reproduction Theory (hereafter SRT) has recently emerged as a vehicle offering social analysis, critique, and strategic political orientation. But what exactly is it? What need does "social reproduction" as a concept respond to, and what theoretical consistency lies beneath the theory's wide-ranging expressions? How do its analytical, critical, and political commitments hang together?

Beyond traditional left circles, there is increasing awareness that anti-capitalism in theory and practice must be informed by women's, anti-racist, Indigenous, anti-colonial and LGBTQIA+ struggles. Migration and disability have also become widely understood as key features when analyzing the harms produced by our class societies. Socially, there is an increasing openness to exploring the ways exploitation must be considered alongside and even a part of so many distinguishable oppressions. Those already organized in left groups are less and less committed to dogmatic economism. These developments are precarious, but have already begun to transform movements for social change.

With roots deepening in response to the growing power of the right around the world, there are substantial gender, race, sex, labor, and immigration status-centered social mobilizations. Black Lives Matter has contested unchecked police violence. Feminist demonstrations have agitated for abortion rights, and against gendered violence. Indigenous struggles have asserted self-determination against resource extraction and pipeline construction. Waves of militant support for immigrants have resisted deportations of migrants through airport shutdowns and disruption of enforcement raids. These campaigns have all generated pointed social analyses that offer theoretical reflections arising from political work. Diverse and radical knowledge has emerged through persistent organizing across these movements. These theories and bodies of knowledge are not limited to the formal teaching and research in academic contexts. Activists share well-crafted reading lists, engage in strategic debates between themselves, and find other means of thinking about struggles and their histories.

As they link insights together, today's radical thinkers can draw on a rich inheritance. From Engels and Zetkin on, Marxist feminists have developed Marx's social theory to criticize social relations that exploit (use workers to grow capital) and oppress (systematically harm some) at the same time.[2] Pioneering theorists helped show how women's oppression is a key to the social relations that capital both shapes and draws on as a resource in its incessant drive to grow.[3] Theories of social reproduction draw from ways Marxist feminists tried to connect women's oppression to exploitation. Insight into these connections are a definitive feature of social reproduction conceptualization and informed strategizing.

But this is not a necessary limit: the basic structure of these theories can often be used to explore and explain other oppressions beyond women's as well. SRT shifts our gaze to concentrate on those agents and forms of work through which abilities to satisfy life's needs are produced, set in motion, and reproduced. Whether training their focus on individuals and their labor power in the family or the enveloping social relations through which different labor powers are produced and reproduced, theories of social reproduction help us see how experiences and histories of oppression and exploitation are mutually determining.

There is increasing openness and desire to develop accounts that tie social movements and labor struggles together. Since 2013, Black Lives Matter emerged in the US not only as an anti-racist struggle, but as an anti-racist struggle with significant class dimensions. Further, activists frequently reminded interpreters who reduced the movement to race alone that the network was itself founded by three Black women, and its stance on queer and trans politics was largely welcoming and liberatory. Likewise, teachers' strikes cannot be understood without attention to their gendered dimensions. As Katie Endicott made clear in the quote at the start of this introduction, coming to see oneself as an "activist" was made possible by the mass involvement of working class women (the majority of public school teachers in every US state). In a similarly gendered vein, finding, maintaining, and reproducing the courage to stand up for "your kids" was crucial for the success of the West Virginia public employee strike of 2018, and Chicago teachers' strike of 2019.

SRT is well-suited to the moment. This is because it is broad enough to recognize and value differing motivations for struggle, yet focused enough to offer a non-reductive anti-capitalist way of unifying them. Through this combination of flexibility and precision, SRT satisfies an emerging theoretical need. As Tithi Bhattacharya has made clear, it achieves this by mapping the class-based harm of exploitation through oppressions, then offering a socialist horizon of emancipation.[4] Socialism here would be both overcoming the social relations that exploit and oppress at the same time, and replacing them with an organization of social relations that is truly conducive to freely developing our needs and capacities.

This book will develop and defend what I take to be the best, most powerful version of SRT. I mean to develop an argument showing that SRT is the best approach at first, grasping the harms suffered in capitalism and second, providing a full-throated justification for socialism. The philosophical reconstruction I offer will show how SRT motivates socialism as the organization of social reproduction most conducive to the benefit of life-making from the standpoint of individual and collective freedom.

But, if SRT is itself a powerful *theory*, why does it need the kind of defense I plan on offering? Can't the existing work, whether movement or scholarly, oriented by SRT speak for itself? What, in other words, might a theoretical defense and justification of SRT amount to? These are not idle or unmotivated concerns. Theory is assumed to be abstract and conducted from a position of privilege. For theory skeptics, it is at best a nice extra flourish, a topping that sweetens. At worst, theory is seen as a distraction from important practical struggles and their study.

When a social theory offers a set of principles to develop a picture of the world, those principles always highlight some parts of the picture while allowing other parts to fall into the background. Different theories provide differing ways of picturing the world and conceiving valuable points of intervention into it. Since there can be different theories, the choice of which theory one works with is actually practically quite important. For instance, consider a social theory offering principles that help explain the necessity of conflict, and assesses agents in terms of political/military formations put in tension by rising and falling powers. This is not a theory we can use to explore the way the division of labor is highly gendered. Likewise, a social theory assuming that hierarchies are divinely ordained or are biologically intrinsic will have a hard time highlighting potential avenues for any revolutionary aspirations of a dominated class.

And this is precisely where the relevance of deepening Social Reproduction *Theory* comes in. Exploring the "theory" of SRT is therefore a way of taking a step back from empirical research, and instead exploring what makes this theory such a coherent and valuable approach. SRT is not, in other words, just one among many frames for developing an understanding of the world. This book argues that SRT's commitment to socialism flows from a frame that develops good, clear-sighted social analysis.

There are three reasons why SRT is so helpful at developing social analyses. The first is that SRT offers a framework that, when put into practice, generates a wide range of accurate analyses. For instance, SRT can be used to zoom in and develop detailed accounts of the family-structured care work in the contemporary context.[5] Or, the theory can zoom out and develop much broader analyses of the capital-inflected changes in how "childhood" is constructed and experienced.[6] Crucially, the theory has the tools to develop rich linkages between these micro and macro levels.

The second reason is that SRT's social analyses can, at the same time, develop social criticism. Standards for criticism are most compelling when they flow not from a knock-down logical argument, but through the norms and values that unfold, even if in frustrated form, in the world that SRT strives to account for. Indeed, SRT is so valuable precisely because its program for research centers the ways our powers are constrained. We are limited to produce and reproduce a very narrow set of values, and often quite oppressive forces.

As Katie Endicott said, teachers caring for "your kids" was made impossible by how states underfunded public schools. SRT works by tracking our needs, how we try to satisfy them, and how we are limited and constrained when other, better, freer possibilities are available. By uncovering avoidable frustrations, tensions, even social contradictions, SRT does more than show what is the case. It shows how what is the case is contradictory, and known or at least knowable as wrong and bad. Since theory is often used to show what's wrong, SRT serves a valuable social function that goes a step beyond providing clear pictures.

The third reason SRT is valuable is its practical consequences. After all, the values of a theory should, at least in part, lie in what it reveals as a task as well as the resources and opportunities to accomplish this task. Of course, many social theories do not aim at tasks, but merely at understanding. SRT, however, is different. Since the theory helps identify the ways our capacities are formed in violent and highly limiting ways, it also points towards a socialist horizon of emancipation.[7]

To develop its argument, the book is developed in seven chapters that build from each other by design. Each chapter, just like this introduction, is preceded with testimony from striking workers involved in either the International Women's Day Strikes (US) or from participants in the wave of public school teachers' strikes. These epigraphs by radical working women motivate the distinct themes of each chapter. They remind us that, ultimately, theory stems from struggle, and has its purchase in how it can help us think about live political problems.[8] The epigraphs are not the results of qualitative research, but serve as points of departure for each chapter and provide real-life motivation for theory. They are often only a few lines from larger stories which deserve careful attention in their own right. I strongly encourage readers to explore these and other interviews and testimonies in full at https://publicseminar.org/author/iwsnyc/ and www.nyctransoralhistory.org/. Though unavoidably condensed, the voices I rely on, to borrow from Patricia Hill Collins, are "both individual and collective, personal and political ... reflecting the intersection of (their) unique biography with the larger meaning of (our) historical times."[9] As stories of working class struggle, I hope they call us to re-commit to pursuing full social emancipation.

To develop social reproduction as a radical framework for social research we can draw on Marx's notion of "labour power." This is understood broadly as the human capacity to actively satisfy needs, and which must be set into motion if any society or individual is to survive. Since labor is needed for production and reproduction, labor power must also be produced and continuously reproduced over time. Both need-satisfying activity and our powers to engage in such activity evolve through work that itself changes as our social conditions and relations change alongside them. In this continuously shifting whole SRT focuses in particular on the changing patterns of labor power. Our powers can grow or decline throughout the day, change over a lifetime, and evolve through the changing strategies we deploy to satisfy social needs.

SRT trains its lens on labor powers and their continuous reproduction. It is not concerned with how many hours of sleep or how many thousand calories are required to get up and go to work each day. Instead, it sheds light on the social inputs that give our powers their particular form. And then, it focuses on the outputs: the way those powers are actually set into motion. It asks what forms of work done by which workers produce labor power, and then what social constraints push those powers to being set in motion (or idled) in various ways. Following Marx, SRT sees labor power as key to producing capital. But it also sees labor powers as the keys to capitalist social relations more broadly. The work people do sets their individual trajectories in motion, and when taken together sets societies in motion as well.

SRT thus widens Marx's lens, expanding the narrow aperture through which the logic of capital's valorization, and *only* this logic, can be seen clearly. By "logic" I mean that we can discern and understand capital's need to continuously expand. I do not mean that this never-tiring demand to grow is itself "rational" or even sensible from the standpoint of human needs or the ecological conditions for the earth's long-term habitability. It is no contradiction to hold that capital's logic is deeply irrational. This logic unfolds in different social environments made up of physical structures and geographies, legal regulations, non-governmental organizations, economic opportunities, state/trans-national apparatus, customs, and histories of oppression and resistance. In short, SRT's framework provides a strong approach to understanding the social forces that generate capitalist social relations, in all their diverse forms.

This focus on labor power makes SRT critical, as well as analytic. Our unrealized potentials to satisfy needs justify criticism. In other words, what labor power *can* do but is constrained from doing leaves us with unmet need, and unmet need can be appreciated as a kind of violence. When a set of social relations develops needs and powers to satisfy them, but simultaneously restrains those powers from being actualized, it can be roundly rejected. SRT shows how the reproduction of labor power is both formed *by* and formative *of* needlessly stunted labor powers. SRT values a wealth of strategies for need-satisfying activity over and against the way capital's narrow demand for self-valorization dominates all other possibilities. And SRT illuminates how capitalism constrains and distorts the development of human powers, thereby preventing them from satisfying our needs. For SRT capitalist social relations not only make and rely on labor powers, they do so in *dis*empowering ways.

Yet, generating a critical perspective from the potentialities of labor power risks making SRT appear beholden to privileging labor in its fully employed, able-bodied, and stereotypically industrial forms. In truth, however, SRT is necessarily committed to rejecting such a position. This is because SRT's criticism of disempowered labor rejects the ways some capacities are sidelined or seen as "disabled" and therefore devalued in capitalist societies.

SRT's commitment to labor power values those capacities that can satisfy human needs here and now. But it also brings into view the emancipatory powers that, when developed and set in motion, would help develop socialism. Capital's profit-driven ableism and productivism can be replaced by a social logic that values the different ways that powers are embodied, and the many different kinds of work people can do. By the same logic, SRT can reject the idea that all powers should be actualized. Carbon-extractive capacities are, for instance, inconsistent with the glaring need to secure habitable ecological conditions. Since our needs are historically and socially changing, what counts as a valuable power is socially determined. SRT accepts neither a promethean overstepping of all bounds nor naturalist determinations of needs and capacities.

Naturalistic strategies are particularly dangerous when used to think the sexed body and women's gender. Yet some prior versions of SRT did move in this direction, or at least opened the door to these kinds of developments. Gender and gender oppression are neither entirely biologically rooted nor a stable, natural existence that was harmed yet could itself serve liberatory ends beyond the violences of capital. Rather, both gender and the multiple forms of gender oppression are something we make. SRT is on firmer footing when it includes gender and the sources of gender oppression, as well as gender resistance, within its account of reproduced powers and social relations. Doing so will make more space to think trans, non-binary, and intersex oppressions and resistances than naturalistic versions of SRT can allow.

Since SRT thinks gender oppressions in relation to class, it is in some ways quite close to intersectional theories. Yet there is often mutual dismissiveness between the two. Marxist social theories have rejected intersectional theories as "bourgeois" for the way they theorize agents through distinct identities, oppressions, or social logics. Others question whether intersectional accounts of oppression have a view of social organization as a whole, whether class is appropriately included in that whole, and whether it has a proper model for how oppressions are combined. Patricia Hill Collins' use of "matrices of oppression" in her development of intersectionality, however, avoids the force of many of these criticisms. Still, there are good reasons to prefer the way SRT develops a notion of class through oppressed powers.

SRT's approach to "class" is valuable because it can combine the logical conception of class with the social forces and lived experiences that flesh it out. The logic of class relations points to the ways society is generally divided. As a Marxist view, SRT distinguishes those who need to exchange their powers for a wage, or rely on those who do, and those who buy labor powers, or otherwise own enough to satisfy their needs. This class division is essential first because it describes the framing conditions for developing and turning powers into activities and second, because this power imbalance is what sets capital on its valorizing paths. The class relation is what permits capital to exploit workers and thereby grow. The logic of the class relation can therefore be understood as the causal or motor force, and one that enables the historical reproduction of capitalist societies.

Yet this absolutely necessary notion of class tells us next to nothing about the specific paths valorization proceeds through. Nor does it account for the wide-ranging forms of social oppression that characterize capitalist societies. For this reason, SRT ties the logical notion of class to other social forces of domination that help determine it. Doing so allows us to see that working class powers are produced and reproduced in ways that are also gendered and racialized, to name just two powerful social forces. SRT can therefore recognize differences within working class populations as essential parts of class experience. Class itself then refers to *both* the logical relation of the working class to the capitalist *and* the set of highly varying and mutable class experiences of working class people.

Since SRT sees the working class as shot through with so many oppressions, it orients struggle towards what I am calling the socialist horizon of emancipation. In this emancipatory sense, "socialism" is nothing other than the set of relations through which powers for need-satisfying activity, and the ways they are reproduced, could be self-guided by the needs of human beings. This provides a way to object to capitalism and the twentieth century's "actually existing socialisms." Both failed to establish the social relations through which developing, actualizing, and reproducing powers would be truly liberating. Socialism is therefore the positive response to manifold disempowerments set into relief by the way SRT pictures the world.

As a horizon of emancipation, socialism must be approached from a given terrain. Meaningful socialist politics follow a grounded appraisal of existing powers. Like any system of social relations, socialism cannot be fully inaugurated and completed in one fell swoop. Like any society, socialism would need to be built and reproduced over time. Yet, the socialist horizon of emancipation is not an infinitely receding horizon, always just beyond reach.

For SRT, socialism is a *political* project. One that requires a clear, class-based strategy for orienting and growing the radical potentials that exist in the here and now. Understanding class in this way shines a light on the necessity of working class solidarity against exploitation not despite, but *through* the working class' differing powers and experiences. To get at the radical potentials of this solidarity SRT asks who reproduces labor powers, and what, beyond labor for capital, these powers can do. The working class is made possible by the class relation, but the powers for socialism are always specifically produced and reproduced through oppressions tied to race, gender, immigrant status, sexuality, ability, and more. Frequently, through their own self-reproduction groups subject to such oppressions develop novel and solidarizing relations that foster radical potentials.

By highlighting the way need-satisfying powers of the working class are formed in impoverishing and constraining ways by capitalist social relations, SRT develops pictures of the world that double as criticisms of it. At the same time, centering these powers provides a clear analysis of the agents who, through solidarity, have the needs and the powers to fight for a radically different, freer and empowering set of social relations.

Finally, a word about Marx. Throughout this book I will be showing how the version of SRT I am developing is a direct development of Marxism. I do not, however, assume that merely showing a theory to be Marxist amounts to an argument for it being a better account than alternatives. While I hold that SRT is an extension of Marxist theory, this is not a dogmatic account which treats Marx's work as a finished article that need only be glossed to arrive at a truth. I rely on brief references to Marx for two different reasons. First, to show those committed to defending Marx that SRT is not a threat, but in fact has its deepest roots in fundamentally Marxist commitments. Second, I quote Marx in elaborating SRT to show readers who enter with a healthy dose of skepticism that Marxist commitments are compelling, even necessary, today.

1

Social Reproduction Theories as Frameworks for Empirical Analysis

My mother is the one who supports me; she is the one who supports all of us. She works as a high fashion dressmaker. Currently she works in a boutique, where she makes bridal dresses—she has always been sewing. My brothers are working too, but … I have more rights because I arrived earlier. They see my mother sick and they do not even take a glass of milk to her; I am the only one who assists her. If her blood sugar goes higher, if she has sudden high blood pressure, I am in charge of checking it and trying to get it lower. Although they see her in pain, they do not even say to her, "Mom, can I help you? Do you need something?" Therefore, I have more rights than them. I am harsher now; I do not know if it is because life made me be like this, but this is how I am. (Nai, on her gendered elder-care and her standing at home)[1]

A VERY BRIEF HISTORY

The need for Social Reproduction Theory then stems from two facts— one social and one theoretical. Socially, it corresponds to the lived, unmet needs produced and then constantly reproduced by gender-differentiating ways of producing frustrated lives dominated by capital. Theoretically, it stems from the fact that a focus on capitalist production alone has failed to provide the resources needed to craft a clear picture that integrates the gendered circuits through which capital passes— particularly the production of embodied labor powers—into an account of how capital reproduces itself in unstable but dominating ways.

The quote from Nai above powerfully illustrates these joint moti-vations. Like her brothers, Nai is a wage-worker, but she also carefully tracks her mother's needs as she reproduces her labor powers. Yet Nai is also expected to do more than a fair share of housework. Nai's expe-rience is far from abnormal, and she explores the possibility that the gender-related extra burdens leveled on her shoulders has made her somewhat harsher. Nai ties her entirely justified frustration to the work she does beyond the fact that, like her brothers, she works for a wage. This is a social reality for Nai, and millions like her. Many social theories are motivated by the need to appreciate burdens tied to but not reducible to being working class, how these burdens have harmful effects, and how they relate to capitalism more generally.

These pressures have pushed some social theorists to adopt dual (or more) systems theories. These tie two or more oppressions to two (or more) distinct causes or logics. However, giving up on a social theory for many partial theories risks never developing an account of how the parts add up to the workings of a whole. Yet, such an account seems necessary if we are to see how distinct forms of oppression operate together in compounding ways. A picture of the whole allows us to craft accounts of their integrations and the underlying motor force that moves oppressions forward in their distinctions, and mutually determining relations.

Developing a comprehensive view of how class and gender relations propel and entrench each other is a long-standing aim of the workers' movement. What today is advanced by Marxist feminists as "unitary theory" follows an impressive legacy of thinking motivated by and interlaced with political struggle. A very brief historical background of what has come to be thought of as "unitary" theories will show how they alone achieve this aim.

Early Marxist feminists recognized that new social relations signaled a need to understand what was referred to as the "woman question." In 1886 Karl Marx's youngest daughter, Eleanor Marx, and her abusive partner Edward Aveling wrote that the "woman question" was first and foremost a question of economic relations. They understood that "the woman question is one of the organisation of society as a whole," and described schisms in nineteenth-century gender politics which still hold today.[2]

When women's movements are dominated by well-to-do women rather than working class women and socialists, upper class points of view prevented them from inquiring into the problems of "society as a whole." Such movements might take some helpful steps in challenging discriminatory laws. But they end up "like doctors who treat a local infection without inquiring into the general bodily health." Well-off women focused on challenging only the most egregious state-backed misogyny which meant: "no attention has been given by them to the study of the evolution of society" as itself a problem for working class women.[3]

For Marx and Aveling, the answer to the "woman question" was growing a working class, women's socialist movement. Theoretical questions about how society and its economic roots evolved in oppressive ways could be posed with a force equivalent to the strength of the working class' pull in the women's movement. The stronger the hard left of the women's movement, the more the capitalist nature of society itself could be recognized as essentially oppressive and thrown into question. This work, however, was only a sketch and at times separated the woman question from an analysis of capital. And even though it was developed as a defense of August Bebel's uneven *Woman and Socialism*,[4] by the end of the nineteenth century early roots of an SRT were apparent.

Ten years later, in 1896, the German Marxist feminist Clara Zetkin began to develop some of the economic analysis Marx and Aveling called for. In a speech to the Party Congress of the Social Democratic Party she said, "it was only the capitalist mode of production which created the societal transformation that brought forth the modern women's question by destroying the old family economic system which provided both livelihood and life's meaning for the great mass of women during the pre-capitalistic period."[5] Once the development of capital pushed women into the workforce, women became reliant on a broader social order for survival. At the same time, women were only integrated into this new, social form of dependence as second class citizens. A women's movement arose which practically and, through the "woman question," theoretically sought to challenge and understand why "the development of her potentials as an individual was strictly limited."

The terms of the so-called "woman question" were sometimes romantically or moralistically phrased. But the contribution of the workers' movement to this debate was an early and significant progenitor to theories of social reproduction. As a powerful question posed by the left, women's oppressions can be charted alongside the radical women's movement's challenges to them. In the Bolshevik's revolution, broader questions of social-economic organization as a whole—and its evolution in oppressive ways—were hotly debated. In the early 1920s the revolutionary Alexandra Kollontai developed a radical feminism that can be read as another early progenitor of SRT.

Kollontai noted how the situation of women changed with the emergence of capitalist social relations. Women became increasingly responsible for earning a wage, performing housework, *and* serving as mothers. In other words, women produced surplus-value for capital and reproduced labor power day to day and inter-generationally. Of course then, "woman staggers beneath the weight of this triple load."[6] Though Nai is not a mother, she does reproduce others' labor powers such that Kollontai's "triple load" fits quite well. Kollontai was careful to mark the distinction between productive work and the other two parts of the triple load she described. Before capitalism, women in agrarian families had access to what they needed to produce for their needs. In the move to capitalism, however, families were separated from what they needed to produce for their needs, and were relegated to activities such as cooking, washing, cleaning, and mending.[7] For Kollontai, that women were somehow still tied to families and forced to do this "unproductive" work was a problem that communism would solve. With the growth of Soviet communism, "the individual household is dying. It is giving way in our society to collective housekeeping,"[8] and, regarding the heavy work of child-rearing, "the collective [is] to assume all the cares of motherhood that have weighed so heavily on women," leaving mothers only "with the smile of joy which arises from the contact of the woman with her child."[9]

In the post-war period, Marxists took their feminist concerns in new directions. Instead of framing the debate in terms of the "woman question," writers and militants became interested in how radical theory and struggle could best understand and respond to different women's oppressions. Claudia Jones was an important, yet often overlooked figure in developing this more nuanced and strategic outlook. In "An End to the Neglect of the Problems of Negro Women!" Jones, writing in 1949, forcefully argued that:

> A developing consciousness of the woman question today … must not fail to recognize that the Negro question in the United States is *prior* to, and not equal to, the woman question; that only to the extent that we fight all chauvinist expressions and actions as regards the Negro people and fight for the full equality of the Negro people, can women as a whole advance their struggle for equal rights … The Negro woman, who combines in her status the worker, the Negro, and the woman, is the vital link to this heightened political consciousness. To the extent, further, that the cause of the Negro woman worker is promoted, she will be enabled to take her rightful place in the Negro proletarian

leadership of the national liberation and movement, and by her active participation contribute to the entire American working class.[10]

By virtue of understanding that the "woman question" needed to be thought of in terms of race as well as class, Jones was grounding Marxist feminism in specific US social conditions.

In Europe, Italian Marxist feminists responded to the changing social conditions of the welfare state. Active in the wages-for-housework campaigns of the 1970s, writers like Mariarosa Dalla Costa created an internal link between women's oppression and capitalism by describing women as beholden to their husband's wage. By reproducing their partner's labor power sexually and through housework, women helped produce men's abilities as commodities for capital. In this way, women indirectly added to the value men produced while at work.[11] Yet, this creative attempt to link women to the production of value tended to rest on two problematic assumptions. The first was the unwarranted assumption that the situation of women could be understood by reading the working class heterosexual housewife as an avatar for all women (something Jones' approach already militated against).[12] The second is that there was something politically regressive in holding onto Marx's idea that some work, even if necessary, does not itself produce value.

Let us return to this question of the "value" of work as a whole. To help make the argument that all work produces value, some theorists relied on an expanded idea of the "social factory." This concept was first developed by Mario Tronti in the Italian workerist movement. Tronti argued that we could see the entirety of capitalist society as producing value since, within it, social relations were all organized to meet this value-producing goal.[13] And Tronti was right, society is indeed organized to produce value. This view also had the virtue of keeping society as a whole in view. In doing so, however, it risked flattening out and denying key distinctions. Just because a whole is best understood in one way, it does not follow that each of the parts that make it up can be understood in the same way.[14] Holding that all social relations produce value because society as a whole is organized to do so denies the specific nature of both "value" and the class relation that makes its accumulation possible. There are also political consequences that stem from the expansive notion of "value" in such a view. If every social relation produces "value," then nearly any form of resistance can be seen as anti-capitalist—even if class relations themselves are not challenged!

This important distinction about "value" was borne in mind and carried forward by later theorists of social reproduction. Although Lise Vogel's seminal *Marxism and the Oppression of Women* first appeared in 1983 it remains an extremely important text. Vogel challenged Italian Marxist feminist and workerist assumptions by centering women's biology. For Vogel, women's *biological* role in the reproduction of labor power from one generation to the next—and not women's day in and day out reproduction of labor powers—is the basis of women's oppression.

By replacing "working class housewife" with the "biologically reproductive" woman Vogel replaced a set of relations with a biological fact. This move, however, supported relational consequences: women's diminished power to produce surplus-value during pregnancy and lactation means women tend to be beholden to men. It is not that biological differences themselves or the division of labor in generationally reproducing labor powers itself is oppressive. Vogel is clear: biological difference is not itself the problem. Biology only becomes a source of oppression because workers must secure their existence via a wage. Not the natural, but the social consequences of women's reproductive biology hinder women's wage-earning. Women's biological role in reproducing labor power inter-generationally, Vogel therefore held, makes women less capable or competitive sellers of labor power than men, and therefore dependent on them. Women as workers are socially produced as impaired workers by capitalist social relations.

The contrast between these theories of women's place in social reproduction can be put more sharply. Where the Italian feminists tended to begin with a one-size-fits-all set of relations figured via the class "housewife", and from that premise tried to account for oppressive social facts, Vogel began with the one-size-fits-all fact of women's sexually reproductive biology. From this premise Vogel integrated capitalist social relations requiring competition in labor markets and developed a framework to describe women's gender oppression. Insofar as both approaches miss the social relations of gendering—through idealization on one side and an over-reliance on biology on the other—these versions of SRT, as foundational as they were, can be improved upon.

In a highly creative approach, Silvia Federici ran both strategies together in 2004 with her highly influential book *Caliban and the Witch*. Federici offered an account of women's oppression as a continuous wellspring of capitalist social relations. For Federici, women had been at the center of freer social relations prior to the emergence of capital. If women were to be fitted into capitalism's oppressive logic of valorization, this gendered freedom had to be constrained and refashioned. The transition to, and the maintenance of, capitalism demanded that women's bodies be reshaped by oppressive logics of production, and reproduction. Women, quite naturally, resisted. And this resistance was met with extreme bodily violence, the paradigmatic example of which was the witch-hunt. For Federici, the one-size-fits-all *fact* was women's natural bodies, while the one-size-fits-all *relations* were violence and resistance.

Configuring women as resistant bodies pushed Federici to a theory of social reproduction that saw capitalist societies as first emerging from and then necessarily hanging on the repeated violation of anti-capitalist women's resisting bodies. In Federici's account, capital both logically and historically requires women's oppression. Despite some historical and logical challenges to her view,[15] the tight fit between theory on one side and vivid social accounts of violence against women and women's heroic resistance on the other has made Federici's theory popular for many left feminists.[16]

Along with the return of so many anti-capitalisms from their banishments as forbidden modes of thinking and politics, socialist feminism is emerging with renewed force. Now the two—socialist liberation and feminism—are increasingly seen as bound to each other. Anti-capitalist projects that do not, at the same time, pursue women's liberation are increasingly rare. From this advanced perspective, theoretical work is trying to catch up with the kinds of unities and solidarities already being set in motion by women's radical struggles. From fighting abortion bans and revanchist regimes, to predominantly women-led public sector strikes, feminism is throwing the social, political, and economic arrangements of capitalism into question.

This resurgence of feminist movements around the globe supports and motivates deepening SRT.[17] In the English-speaking world, where struggle is less developed, it is perhaps no surprise then that there has been a resurgence of interest in the theoretical side of SRT.[18] These explorations have the virtue of combining theoretical developments with wide-ranging material analyses, all situated by sharp political orientations. A remaining task for SRT is to offer a compelling theoretical synthesis, one providing the resources to situate these and so many other flourishing articulations of SRT. Combining economic and social theory in a way that sees, objects to, and opens a horizon of emancipation beyond oppression is not, however, a small task. What follows in this book therefore cannot possibly hope to end the conversation on SRT. As Eleanor Marx knew, theoretical questions will be taken up and sharpened as liberatory movements gain direction from the working class. As a step in that direction, the conversation can be pushed forward by bringing to light some of SRT's underlying radical potentials.

PRODUCTION, REPRODUCTION, AND THE *THEORY* OF SOCIAL REPRODUCTION

Marxists often think about production, that is, how we organize work and what it actually accomplishes. This question of production is often featured in discussions around social reproduction as well. Production is peculiar, however, because, at least in capitalist societies, what we produce does more than satisfy social needs. In satisfying some need what is produced often grows capital by adding "value." In this way then, the Marxist sense of the term "productive activity" holds that some work also produces "value."

Holding that value is *made* means that in capitalism, value is never a simple fact about the world, nor something we immediately inhabit. Nor even is value a direct expression of our desires and preferences, as when we value honesty, the way we are embodied, affection, or courage. The Marxist account of value describes the production of value in an economic sense. Value is measured by the surplus (or extra) that returns to capital beyond its expenditure. It is, in other words, the growth of capital after accounting for all expenses in production. In the capitalist system, production takes place for the sake of capitalist value, that is, for the expansion or "valorization" of capital itself. Ecological and social needs are only met if, through doing so, production can valorize capital, that is, expand its value.

For capital to grow in value, certain social relations must be in place. At the very basis of things, the workers must be separated from what it takes for us to work. And then, crucially, capital orchestrates a peculiar kind of return to production in the coordination of what had been separated. Without access to what it takes to produce, and thereby satisfy our own or anyone else's needs, would-be workers need to exchange our powers to produce for a wage. Workers then use the wage to satisfy needs. The result is that on the basis of this division (and then this wage-motivated coordination) capitalism sets otherwise frustrated powers for productive activity into motion for the sake of producing capitalist value.

This framework means that Marxists have a specific circuit in mind when using the word "value." The things we need and the values we hold, even under capitalism, can be "valuable" in a very broad sense without producing "value" in the narrower, capital-focused sense. "Value" as referring strictly to the surplus that returns to and expands capital after accounting for costs is a rather odd and capital-specific way of determining value. It is far from intuitive. It may be helpful to think of this as what is valuable from the perspective of capitalism, rather than those forced to live through it.

For example, writing a good poem or caring for a family member in need, as Nai does, are activities which are, without doubt, valuable in some sense. We need poetry, caring relations, and the time to do both without guilt or sacrifice. Often, the violence done to our lives when our existence depends on exchanging our powers for a wage makes us value whatever access we have to art and care even more. Yet, what is important here is that from the standpoint of the expansion of capitalist value, neither writing a poem nor caring for a family-member is considered "productive." Following Marx's definition,[19] time spent on these valuable activities does not make the surplus-value that capital needs. Obviously then, the notion of what activities are "productive" in the Marxist sense is rather narrow. What is "productive" in this sense is limited by the standpoint of capital. Value is measured in capital's growth, rather than in terms most of us would recognize. This capitalist way of conceiving things really focuses on, and is therefore only concerned with, its own value-expansion. It is compelled, at great ecological, personal and social cost, to find more and more avenues to produce surplus-value, to grow.[20]

Capitalism pursues this limitless, never-ending process because the failure to do so entails devastating consequences. Given rough competition, capitalists may lose their means of production, and fall from the more comfortable life of a capitalist into the less comfortable life of a worker. Though narrow in one sense, this definition is also absolutely essential to understand how capital works. It helps us appreciate the basic logic of all capitalist societies, because it points to the motive force incessantly beating at the very heart of each one.[21] That is, the unavoidable imperative to maximally grow surplus-value, to compete—and win—in the race to valorize at the highest rate possible. Yet the race never ends. As long as the class relation pushing this kind of production persists—workers separated from what we need to satisfy our needs—this heartbeat of valorization persists.

This value-growing process is also very specific and flows through other social relations. And these vary according to the histories and places of so many quite different capitalist societies. The problem with an abstract view of value is that in its abstraction it cannot center the specific social relations through which valorization takes place. It needs to be fleshed out because we know nothing about the social forces, syncopated rhythms, or varying speeds of valorization from the realization that capital is always engaged in a process of valorization.

A more complete understanding of capital should link this central beating heart of valorization to social analyses of the evolving cycles and social circuits that capital moves through as it valorizes. The problem is not that there is something wrong or unhelpful in Marxist notions of value, what counts as "productive" of it, and why value's logic motivates constant expansion. Quite the opposite. It is precisely *because* these ideas single out something shared and appropriate to each and every possible capitalist society that they can help us. Appreciating the internal working of value allows us to understand the underlying logic of any capitalist society. The degree of abstraction in these ideas is essential to finding something shared across tremendously diverse capitalist societies. Yet the strength of this universality comes at a steep cost. Value-centered concepts do little on their own to flesh out the bare logic that they describe.[22] They cannot help us see why some people have to choose between poetry and care work, why some don't seem to face that forced choice, and more pointedly, why still others experience neither poetry nor care work as conceivable choices in the first place.

It's obvious that a value-centered account is limited. In order to provide more specific and grounded accounts of value's role in particular contexts, we would need to study actual social relations, as well as their histories. We would need to trace out how these relations set some labor powers into value-productive motion, while some labor powers are set into motion without producing value, while still others are oppressively constrained from their possible activity. We need to study how these tendencies, taken together, aid capital's valorization in socially divergent, and often very irregular, heartbeats. We then need to return and connect these more specific accounts with capital's underlying logic: the valorization appropriate to any capitalist system.

One might say that the narrower notion of what produces value is fairly empty until it has been fleshed out with the social relations that obtain in a given context. And the specific social contexts are blindly uncoordinated until they are sharpened, and given direction by an underlying logic. Taken together, we would have a fleshed out logic. And finally, we would have the makings to develop a fine account not just of capital in the abstract, but of capitalist societies in their lived, unfolding forms.

Putting these two perspectives—the logical and the social—together into a unitary framework stitches together an underlying logic with the concrete realities of so many different social organizations. It allows our theory to explain how the two perspectives interact, influence and contribute to the reproduction of each other over time. We can then carefully avoid reducing one to the other. This would be the case if, for instance, we held that the *function* of care work and the women, like Nai, who disproportionately do it is to create a class of workers that capital can exploit. Capital does require that labor powers be reproduced, and labor powers do require significant care. But rendering care work as if it were a mere function of capitalism would ignore its specifics as an industry as well as all its other effects.

SRT can recognize that what is functional from the narrow standpoint of capital valorization is not the only way to understand social activities (or even necessarily the best one). Such a narrow account would miss the chance to explain why women and immigrants tend to do the kind of care work that Nai does. This view would also miss that there are other values at play than those intelligible from the standpoint of capital's "value." And at least one goal of a liberatory theory is to make other values intelligible and legible, despite their marginalization at the hands of narrow and oppressive logics because, in the end, we can do a lot more with our powers than simply grow capital.

The other side of seeing everything we do as a function for capital valorization would be denying that capital's valorization is, in reality, an objective and indeed leading social force. By focusing on the differences between capitalist societies, the different ways capitals influence different workers (say, construction workers, poets, and elder-care workers), or by holding that capital has no purchase on certain kinds of work (the uncompensated care of a family member in need), some social theories risk understating the centrality of valorization.

The version of SRT developed here is helpful because it provides the tools to avoid both pitfalls. It allows us to understand the force of capital's imperative to valorize, while directing our gaze to research on the specific ways that gender, race, sexuality, immigration status, and other oppressions form the particular social paths through which valorization takes place.[23] Social reproduction theorists are aware that valorization requires labor powers set in motion, and that this motion is premised not just on the bald *fact* that workers are separated from the means of production. Crucially, it is premised on the actual ways workers are separated from the means of production in different and historically changing patterns.

Frequently the two approaches to social theory are combined. This is the case, for instance, when paying attention to how reproducing the labor power at the basis of capital's valorization is a highly gendered task. Empirical research has repeatedly shown that, for all the women's movement's breakthroughs, heterosexual couples tend to burden women with the majority of domestic work. When social reproduction theorists explore the ways women tend to be charged with the un- or under-compensated work that makes workers capable of going back to work day in and day out, they tend to develop two key claims. First, this work of reproducing our embodied labor powers is absolutely essential to the function of any capitalist society. Capital cannot valorize without setting labor powers in motion.[24]

What is crucial to note here is that this work of preparing embodied labor powers for the market is done predominantly by *women*. And thus the social realities of valorization, and the conditions that make capital valorization possible, are far from gender-neutral. It is not that the abstract logic of valorization is itself a gendered process. After all, how could it be if the abstract logic of valorization is developed by abstracting *away from* gender and, in particular, the ways gendering links up with working? Rather, social reproduction theorists tend to mark how valorization proceeds through gendered circuits. This process creates inequalities which then serve as breeding grounds and magnifiers for persistent inequalities within the working class.[25]

Following the second insight, SRT sometimes focuses on the social relations and consequences of these unevenly distributed opportunities for "productive" work. There are real social consequences to not having access to the means of production. It is the basis of class relations—in which one is either a buyer or seller of labor power. But there are further consequences to lacking access to the means of production *while also* facing social inequalities that make it harder to develop or exchange labor powers for a wage. SRT provides a framework to chart how the reproduction of the working class is at the same time the reproduction of gendered (as well as many other) distinctions within it.

The analysis endorsed by SRT then often contrasts value-productive work with socially reproductive work. And social reproduction theorists can rely on Marx to help draw the distinction between work that is "productive" and all the other work that makes the production of capitalist value possible. It is not as simple as dividing workers or forms of work into two neatly opposed sides. After all, someone working for a wage in a for-profit elder-care home will perform some of the exact same tasks that Nai does in her own home without pay.[26] When Nai does it at home it is socially reproductive without producing capitalist value while elder-care workers in for-profit settings engage in socially reproductive work that also produces capitalist value. The production of value and the reproduction of capital (and its prerequisites) offer two subtle, but importantly distinct grounds for theorizing. They offer two different ways of seeing the world.

The value-productive approach asks about the kinds of work and the kinds of working conditions that produce surplus-value. It tries to figure out how capital as a regime of value production is organized. To return to the metaphor, it is interested in the structure of the heart, the quality, and the nature of its beat. Logically and empirically, this approach tends to look into the relations engendered by separating workers from the means of production. It explores how labor powers bought by a wage and set into actual motion produce surplus-value. It therefore tends to work with the narrower notions of value and production described above. Since value is the heart of capitalist societies, adopting this approach would be like seeing the human body from the perspective of a cardiologist.

Analyzing capitalism through the lens of SRT does not require denying the specific logic of value production (even if, at times, some articulators of SRT have done just that).[27] The theory is on firmer footing when it focuses on how value production historically persists and grows capital in unstable, oppressive, and even contradictory ways. A socially reproductive approach recognizes that capital's valorizing logic is temporal and always housed in a social organization that reproduces itself. Accounts of capital are therefore stronger when, in addition to uncovering capital's logic, they develop social and historical analyses as well. Since the truth of valorization is necessarily a social and time-related truth, concrete social-historical analyses are indeed necessary. To stick with the medical analogy, those adopting the SRT approach can be likened to general internists—concerned with the whole body, its history, and the complex connections between different organs and systems.

In this light, SRT tracks the changing social realities that enable and condition capital's foundational logic of valorization. SRT can then offer a materialist history of social relations, one that recognizes the changing dynamics that condition all the possibilities to work. It can track the specific nature and relation between work that produces capitalist value and work that does not. What should be clear here is that capital's imperative to valorize is only possible through so much work that does not directly produce value. As a result, a narrow focus on value-productive work provides only partial and incomplete understanding of capitalist society. We would certainly be missing a lot about capitalism if the only thing we thought was important to understand about Nai is the fact that she also works outside the home for a demolition company.

The range of social relations and work to be explored by SRT is therefore tremendously wide-ranging. Yet it is not, for this reason, forced to offer nothing more than a random hodge-podge of disconnected social reflections. The way societies are reproduced across time as capitalist is the common thread uniting such a variable approach.[28] SRT thus provides a social account of capital which, since it is an account of *capital*, recognizes the central and guiding force of the imperative to produce surplus-value.

Situating the logical imperative historically is crucial for political analysis. This is because the separation from productive powers that compels labor power to exchange itself for a wage did not spring from thin air. We cannot simply assume this separation as ahistorical and permanently fixed. It is, in fact, first established and then socially reproduced as an ongoing condition for capitalist production. This historical separation was accomplished around the world at different points in time, in vastly different ways, with even more vastly different social consequences. And these consequences evolved through the new, distinctly capitalist form of social reproduction. While still inflected by previous era's oppressive dynamics, these newer forms are fundamentally organized and set in motion by the historically achieved, but politically challengeable capitalist relations.

Like anything that is socially reproduced, the story can be changed going forward. The fact that we are not as free as we would like to be to make such changes does not mean that our past histories are unavoidable, future destinies. As Ursula Le Guin said in her national book award speech, "We live in capitalism. Its power seems inescapable. So did the divine right of kings."[29] Capital's logic of valorization can be put to a halt by stopping any activities necessary for accumulation, whether productive of value or not. As any good elder-care worker knows, a blood clot in the legs can be just as deadly as a clot in the heart. By stressing the historical unfolding of reproduction, the SRT framework allows us to see that production itself does not need to be organized around the basic capitalist imperative to grow surplus-value. We should not forget that private ownership of the means of production emerged only recently given the vast scope of human history. And even then, private ownership has already been successfully resisted or overcome many times, and in many places. Anything that requires our power to be reproduced can be produced in different ways, or not at all.

A challenge for SRT then emerges when we take up these political insights. Broadened in this way to include both the expansion of value, as well as the social and historical relations that render such expansion possible, the very concept of social reproduction may seem to lose its specificity and political edge. Marx himself even seemed to conflate production and reproduction when in *Capital* he wrote, "When viewed ... as a connected whole, and as flowing on with incessant renewal, every social process of production is, at the same time, a process of reproduction. The conditions of production are also those of reproduction."[30]

If social reproduction includes the production of value, how can we keep the two apart for the purposes of analysis, and action? What is the specific object that SRT intends to study? Consider the production of space that will be used to create elder-care homes. In this case we see the reproduction of construction workers through their wages, as well as capitalist valorization. And in such work, further distinctions are reproduced as well: as Nai described in her interview, in demolition work women are tasked with doing the clean-up work more than men.

The production of value embodied in buildable lots for elder-care homes reproduces one part of the construction industry, the workers themselves, gendered distinctions within the workers, distinctions between all workers and their capitalist bosses, as well as a culture of making distinct spaces for the care that we need as we age. All productions of value are in some sense social. For that reason, value production is also in some sense reproductive of the social relations through which capital valorizes.[31] Indeed, for Marxists, analytic distinctions can always be traced back to distinguishable parts set in relation to each other within a broader social totality.[32]

It is hard to maintain a firm boundary between production on one side and reproduction on the other. While perhaps analytically satisfying, this divide would be conceptually cutting the world into pieces that are needlessly difficult to link back together again in a coherent and readable picture. But it is important that the commitment to seeing production as part of reproduction does *not* mean the opposite is also true. It is not the case that *every* act of reproduction is also, at the same time, productive of value in the narrower sense.

"Social reproduction" is therefore best understood not as a term singling out some distinct content, but as a framework for investigating and understanding the world, with particular attention to the way our embodied labor powers are made and sustained. SRT is then at its strongest when it refuses to curtail its view by focusing on only one group of workers, or only one kind of work, and instead situates the highly gendered work of reproducing embodied labor powers in light of a broader social totality riven by many forms of oppression. The strongest accounts of SRT follow interlocking forms of labor: identifying unfolding relations between workers and their world as their power to make it is directed by the pressure of capital.

TOWARDS A UNIFIED FRAMEWORK

A unified framework for empirical analyses could not possibly draw on and try to synthesize the entire history of SRT. Only a small sample of its genealogy and breadth could be glossed over in the preceding pages. This breadth included some versions that were directly at odds with others, and some starting assumptions no longer (if they ever really did) help provide the clear vision of society that we need today.

In addition, a unified framework is merely the scaffolding for, and could never itself be a complete, social analysis. Still, a unified framework for SRT can provide the guidelines through which a whole can be kept in view and how, in light of the whole, parts—like gender and immigration status, race, ability, and class—can be linked up to each other. Fine-grained research programs into the specifics remain absolutely necessary, and no research project should be considered insufficient because it cannot do everything all at the same time.[33] SRT provides an essentially integrative framework, providing a unifying focus through which we can examine details concerning parts of the whole. For that reason, SRT should exclude no social arenas from its possible view. In principle,

SRT can welcome with open arms diverse disciplines and methods of investigation. Sociological, anthropological, economic, political, ecological, and geographical approaches, not to mention their more abstract approach in philosophical work, can all be mutually enriching means of developing and then using a social reproduction framework.[34]

SRT can integrate any research that helps us understand the powers, activities, and relations of reproduction as part of an overarching capitalist social order. Though consistent in the sense of always demanding surplus-value, this order is far from consistent in the sense of being homogenizing or levelling. The production of surplus-value, and the social relations that enable and then reproduce valorization as an imperative, are made and experienced in different ways in different places by different people. The lived experiences of both production and social reproduction re-inscribe differences in our ecological conditions and social fabric that evolve yet persist over time. As such, a unified framework should be able to situate the ways gender, race, nationality, immigration status, ability, and so many other kinds of differentiation, are turned into forms of oppression through capitalist production and reproduction without construing any of the sources of oppression as natural or fixed.[35]

As it has in the past, a social reproduction lens can develop a feminist politics but it can just as easily think about other and inter-connected oppressions.[36] And it should. For the unified frame to do its integrative work, social reproduction feminism and its concerns with women's oppressions needs to be both deepened and broadened. It needs to be deepened so it can appropriately theorize situations like Nai's. In addition to being a woman, Nai is an immigrant woman, without full legal standing in the (US) state she resides and works in. On the other hand, social reproduction feminism needs to be broadened, or at least open to linking up with the issues raised by disability rights movements, and not only because Latin Americans are deeply over-represented among those hurt in the construction industry.[37]

What I have called SRT's variable lens is therefore responsible for doing more than amassing a collection of differently detailed pictures. The variable lens also needs to be capable of providing a 360° view. Feminisms that have left out immigration and race by implicitly assuming white women who are also citizens were quite appropriately criticized for working with a reductive and marginalizing model that captures far less than they intend.[38] The social analyses sponsored by their theories leave already oppressed women out of their picture. Finally, any socially reproductive lens needs to be capable of capturing not just the nature of such oppressions, but their change through time.

To say, as SRT does, that we reproduce society is not only to name an unevenly distributed burden. It is also to say that we are the social agents producing and reproducing our opportunities and powers to change these structuring realities in the future. This means that, even when not functioning as social "activists," we are agents for social construction and crucially, agents of social change. How we work, refuse to work, or are prevented from working in trying to satisfy our needs is socially formative and transformative. These are the paths through which we first develop and then actualize our powers by setting them into motion. Sue Ferguson developed the immense breadth of this insight by calling all such activity "life-making." This "life-making" refers to individual lives not as mere individuals, but as tied to the societies through which individuals are situated and maintained.[39] On this notion of individuality, then, to say that we are life-making is also to say that we have some powers to shape and reshape the social reproduction of life.[40]

At the level of the individual, in addition to a bundle of commodities and the wage needed to acquire that bundle, we share basic needs. We all need love, patience, respect, education, encouragement, and guiding criticism. We need these, and so much more. We have the need to fulfill our lives on our own terms not simply because without them our labor power would be under-developed or less competitive. Yet just as no one is born with labor power to sell, no one is born with robust abilities for love, respect, poetry, encouragement, guidance, and so many other truly valuable social powers. Our powers to satisfy our needs are then central to every aspect of production and reproduction, including the production of social organizations beyond capitalism. How SRT thinks "power" in this wide-ranging sense is crucial to its success as a basis for political strategy. What SRT means by "power" is then the main focus of the next chapter.

2

Power as Potentiality or the Critical Dimension of Labor Power

More than anything I left my country because I wanted to get out to learn something new. I came with the desire to study but it became a bit difficult. I came to realize that the situation is difficult for people who don't have paper who want to study. I wanted to be a computer programmer. I had taken some courses in that in Argentina. But because of the language barrier, because I didn't have papers, and because I'm all alone here (I was the first in my family to come) I had to decide if I was going to work or study and, well, I had to work. I didn't have a choice. (Ana, on how the free development of her powers was constrained)[1]

The preceding overview suggested that Social Reproduction Theory's commitments point to liberatory projects. If we continuously make and remake our world, ourselves, and the relationships between the two, how we have the ability to do this is crucially important if we are to flesh out SRT's emancipatory potentials. To answer this question, social reproduction theorists pay close attention to what we may think of as our formative powers. From a Marxist perspective, these capacities are our "labour powers." They can be set in motion or restrained from being actualized, as is the case when one is unemployed, lacks sufficient means of production beyond employment, or when one intentionally withholds the powers through striking or other work stoppages. In what follows I will unpack the scope and meaning of "labour powers," and develop them as the key to SRT's criticism of capital.

To be more concrete, Ana has the power to study computer programming—she already did so in Argentina. In the US, however, Ana is not free to actualize her power to study. But powers are broader than their actualizations. No one would deny that Ana's ability to study still exists. If conditions were different her power *could* be actualized, which means the capacity is still there. The powers to study, read, care for the elderly, write poetry, demolish buildings, or to make any number of commodities all exist in any event, even when they are not actively being set into motion.

The list is quite broad, so we might ask: What counts as a labor power? The term conjures images of muscle-bound, masculine workers using their potencies in construction, demolition, or other heavy industries.[2] However, in a world where women's labor is serially under-respected— when not outright ignored—and social power is disproportionately wielded by men, we can see where this limited and limiting image comes from. Characterizing labor power in such a way really risks blinding us to the extraordinary diversity of labor powers.

Given the way this image has dominated for so long it may be surprising to notice that, for Marx, nearly anything can count as a labor power. In *Capital*, he provides the following definition: "By labour power or capacity for labour is to be understood the aggregate of those mental and physical capabilities existing in a human being which he (sic) exercises whenever he produces a use value of any description."[3] There are a few things to notice about this expansive account. First, this definition tells us that labor powers are not simply those powers that, when set in motion, create surplus-value for capital. The notion of labor powers being used here is much broader. Labor powers are those capacities that produce everything that we find valuable— "a use value of any description" means nearly anything useful at all.[4]

Since use-values are of *any* description, they can include useful things besides the commodities that transform labor powers into profits for capital. It is only under conditions of capital that workers are forced to expend their labor powers in ways that make capital valorize. As Marx writes, capitalists want to "produce not only a use value, but a commodity also; not only use value, but value; not only value, but at the same time surplus value."[5] Humans have always worked to make useful things, and most societies create surpluses. But we have not always performed this work under the same social conditions. In capitalism production is arranged to make use-values if they are, at the same time, vehicles for capital's valorization. To quote Marx again:

> The labour process, resolved as above into its simple elementary factors, is human action with a view to the production of use values … it is the everlasting nature-imposed condition of human existence, and therefore is independent of every social phase of that existence, or

rather, is common to every such phase ... As the taste of the porridge does not tell you who grew the oats, no more does this simple process tell you of itself what are the social conditions under which it is taking place, whether under the slave-owner's brutal lash, or the anxious eye of the capitalist, whether Cincinnatus carries it on in tilling his modest farm or a savage (sic) in killing wild animals with stones.[6]

Marx's idea is that labor powers are, in a sense, trans-historical. Though specifically determined in every historical period, labor powers are themselves the kinds of things that humans always have. Our powers will vary across time and space, but the fact that we have some labor powers is the kind of fact that will always be true. Now, while labor powers can be formed and put to use by capital, any social organization—including non-capitalist ones—requires some version of labor powers. This is required if the organization is to produce the useful things that it needs to reproduce itself over time.

Marx is indeed clear that labor powers exist in ancient and feudal societies, not just in the commodified form that capital generates. As he notes: "to find labour power offered for sale as a commodity, various conditions must first be fulfilled."[7] Before those conditions were in place, labor power was a feature of a wide range of pre-capitalist historical societies. "Greek society," Marx holds, "was founded upon slavery, and had, therefore, for its natural basis, the inequality of men and of their labour powers."[8] The key point here is that labor powers can be configured in tremendously different ways, across vast stretches of time—from ancient Greece's slave societies to nineteenth-century Europe's in which labor powers could be offered for sale as a commodity.

There is a nearly hidden idea in Marx's thought about labor powers in ancient Greek society. Marx suggests that the inequality of powers went hand in hand with the fact that everyone possesses some. Though not part of the producing classes, Greek slave-holders *also* had labor powers. These capacities were set into motion in ways that satisfied the needs of a patrician life. After all, Greek aristocrats were also human beings with mental and physical capacities. They too set processes in motion to create useful things, at least for themselves. For Marx, any power at all for creating something we could use counts as a labor power. So it follows that Greek slaves, free craftsmen, and aristocrats all possessed versions of labor power, though of course in vastly different and clearly unequal ways.

In capitalist societies, it also makes sense to think of capitalists as having their own labor powers. This is not because their exercise of such powers gives them much in common with the working class. Quite the opposite. Rather, capitalists must have some labor powers if we are to think of their activity as producing something that is useful in some sense. Even if it is only their decadent lives, Marx's broad notion of "labour-power" as that which "produces a use-value of any description" is spacious enough to include capitalists' powers as well. The definition amounts to having some kind of potency for acting in a useful way, and "use" can be very broadly conceived.

We know capitalists have some labor powers given what happens when, as frequently does happen, they fail as capitalists. If upon their failure it is possible for capitalists to work, then some labor powers must have been lying dormant. It would be silly to think that these powers suddenly emerge at the very moment a failing business is forced to liqui-date its means of production, and the owner becomes working class. But this does not mean that everyone is implicitly a member of the working class. Nor does it mean that capitalists' powers should be respected or that they produce value in the Marxist sense. It simply means that everyone has powers to labor to create things that are, in some sense, useful. Nothing about this universality of labor powers should be under-stood as denying that under capitalism, one's class position sets the rails for how such powers are developed and actualized (or not).[9]

It should also be relatively easy to motivate the idea that labor powers *are*, which is to say, they exist even when they are not formally exchanged for a wage or actualized without any compensation. Our potentials are always and unavoidably deeper and broader than the ways they are actualized. When one could work but does not, either because one is on strike, taking a break, or has not, or not yet, been hired to do so, the power to work remains. Unemployed people have labor powers, but these powers are generally not useful enough for capital to set them in motion. Strikers have labor powers too. Striking is therefore the act of withholding pure labor power itself as a weapon in the class struggle.

But what of powers in their exhaustion? After a long day at work, laborers can be tired out. As social reproduction theorists center so well, powers are spent in the course of the day and so must be reproduced for the next one. No one—not even Stakhanov—can work indefinitely without a break.[10] Labor powers are minded and embodied. But both the mind and body only have a certain amount of energy which means they can be exhausted, and often are. The course of our activity is almost never identical with the replenishment of our ability to act. This may seem like a simple point, but there are actually a few distinct issues at play. The first is the fact of energy—being tired or being entirely exhausted sets a limit to how long we can actively engage our labor powers. Beyond the period of inactivity—the rest and sleep that everyone needs—we have other needs as well. We aren't like automatic vacuums that simply need one thing, and recharge to get it when not in action.

This points to the much more specific and socially varying set of things that we need to replenish our powers. Personally, it would be nearly impossible to put in a day of work without coffee in the morning. Marx famously required a steady supply of brandy and cigars as a condition for his work, and he was happy to consider socially determined consumer needs like tobacco as necessities required for the maintenance of the working class.[11] From clothes, diet, and what we smoke to bonding and cultural experiences, what we need to reproduce labor powers varies tremendously, according to time and place.[12]

Labor powers can then be thought about in at least two different senses. The question can be posed more philosophically, as when we try to understand what labor powers are in and of themselves. As we've already seen, nearly all human beings have them. From here, we can explore what it means when we hold that human beings are the kinds of beings that have labor powers—in any configuration. A philosophical answer to that question offers what is sometimes called a "philosophical anthropology." This is a reasoned account of what in general the category human refers to— and SRT would tie such an account to these labor powers.

Sometimes such an account is thought of as an account of "human nature." But the very concept of a "nature" is at least a little suspect. It seems to suggest that the account to follow would provide some list of fixed, supposedly "natural" facts. Such a conception of human nature, however, runs against the stress SRT places on the social and historical processes of becoming. SRT explores ways of producing and reproducing powers that change over time and place, and which respond to and develop different sets of needs. For this reason, a "philosophical anthropology" appropriate to SRT is far more socio-historical than "natural."

Perhaps it helps to think of our nature itself as socio-historical. This version of our "nature" would signify something that is continuously in the process of being transformed both socially and historically through our activity. For this reason too, SRT's focus on the essentially changing nature of our labor powers provides some fine resources to respond to charges of essentialism. If what we are by "nature" is social, historically different and always changing, then SRT's philosophical anthropology also has a unique potential. It can provide us with resources to respond to the false universalisms of Eurocentrism, white-centrism, hetero-normativity, and other narrow prejudices that have been the appropriate objects of criticism.

In addition to developing a philosophical anthropology, the second way to approach the question of labor powers at the center of SRT is to pose it in a less abstract, more concrete way. The philosophical approach asks what it means to hold that humans are the kinds of beings that have labor powers of some kind. And so a more concrete approach would instead ask questions like: Where do the labor powers that we do have come from? What arrangements actually produce and sustain them here and now? How and why do some societies, like our own and the ancient Greek ones, arrange these powers in extremely unequal ways? And, more forcefully, why are some of us here and now more free to develop and actualize our powers than others? Or, why are some powers less easy to develop and more constrained such that they are limited to remaining only potentials for action? And finally, most importantly, how and to what extent might constrained powers open up space to challenge the very social dynamics of their constraint?

A PHILOSOPHICAL ANTHROPOLOGY OF LABOR POWERS—THE POSSIBILITY OF SOCIAL CRITICISM

Like any philosophical anthropology, one rooted in seeing us as historical beings with labor powers will be more theoretical than concrete. The value of the abstraction stems from how a step back helps situate lived realities in a coherent and, ultimately, a *critical* way. When we see labor powers as an essential part of what it means to be human, we can forcefully object to the ways that our powers are constrained—instead of freed up—by our social organization. But there are a few steps before the critical thought can be fully earned.[13]

First, to hold that individuals are beings with labor powers, in the plural, is to hold that we are the kinds of beings that have *various* powers. We are not fated to act only in accordance with one immediately given, and primarily motivating, power. That would amount to reducing us to our instincts. We are, to be sure, *also* instinctual beings. We feel the pull of hunger and thirst like so many other animals. But how we end up satisfying these instinct is determined by the choices we make.

To say that we have many different powers then is also to say that we are free. But this is true only in a limited sense. We are not free to do whatever we want—say fly like a bird, live like an ancient Greek, or study everything we want all at the same time—but we do have some scope of freedom. When setting and pursuing our goals we have at least some space to choose which goals to set and just how we are going to pursue them. We have some space to make decisions, and to be intentional. Since we can recognize and choose amongst different strategies for need-satisfying activity, we have some space to make plans. This is a rich notion of "freedom" because it makes freedom both a fact and something that we have to actively realize. Freedom is not fully given, but instead something we accomplish in the world when we set our capacities to satisfy our needs into motion.[14] In this light, freedom can be widened or fashioned in a more blinkered way—depending on the scope of our powers and the ways we can relate to them.

The diversity and freedom of labor powers correspond to the fact that we *do not* have what we need already at hand. We are not like plants, capable of absorbing what we need directly from our environment. Nor are we like a perfect god, whose perfection would amount to having no needs in the first place. We use our powers and our freedom to satisfy needs only because we are, in the first place, already and unavoidably needy beings.[15] If we are needy and do have some freedom through some powers to satisfy our needs, then we are not obliged to fatefully accept what is meted out by an all-providing god. Nor do we have to stoically identify with the pain of unmet need. An approach which includes needs and capacities for their satisfaction as an indispensable feature of human life can avoid these pitfalls.

This emphasis on neediness puts the lie to liberal, individualist notions of self-sufficiency by drawing out the truth of our social dependence. Both our needs and our possibilities for fulfilling them are produced and reproduced socially. Our capacities are not just *for* social existence, they stem *from* our social existence, and refract back on it. This is clear given the fact that we have social needs ourselves.[16] It is also clear from the fact that labor powers are generationally and individually produced through the indirect efforts of social communities. Further, in capitalist societies workers are socially dependent on bosses for a wage and bosses are dependent, though not symmetrically, on labor powers for their surplus-value. Even our need for isolation is socially influenced in that the desire for some privacy from social connections is itself socially conditioned.

This is not to say that all powers are social powers in the sense that, rather than belonging to individuals themselves, they actually belong to the society that envelops and situates individuals. Society itself is not a "labor power," nor does society itself exercise "labor powers." On Marx's definition, only individuals develop labor powers. But we all do so in ways that are shot through with social implications. In ancient Greece, for instance, society was forcefully arranged around slave-labor and the relations of inequality that kept that violent mode of production stable. In capitalism today, society is no less forcefully arranged around the production of labor powers, although its stability is frequently subject to crisis.[17] Society itself organizes our labor powers and conditions the paths and powers of our individuation. Society is therefore both the path for our differential empowerments and again, in different ways, limits their flourishing.

SRT then complicates the ideal picture of individuals as independent, autonomous beings. In improving upon liberal notions of individuality, however, SRT does not have to do away with "individuality" all together. Acknowledging that our powers are socially conditioned does not amount to rejecting the very idea of an "individual" as if it were a fiction. It simply means our individuality is social: we are social individuals, and we are socially individuated. Individuals contribute to—and are situated within—a set of social forces which are themselves powerful determinants shaping our life-making powers.

To understand the contemporary state of labor power, we must illuminate a particular form of domination. Under conditions of capital, the social individuation of our labor powers flows through the labor markets where so many of us have to sell these powers. Here our powers get measured in terms of a wage and become, in this sense, commensurate or exchangeable commodities. The uniqueness of our powers, the specific way we acquired them and the way they are embodied in us, as well as the different ways they may be realized are all flattened out. They are inevitably reduced to a common denominator—the going rate offered, the wage. Worse still, they are all commodified as *buyable* via such a wage.

Being employed is an ambivalent condition: it at once advantages us socially, but it also exposes us to exploitation. Yet this ambivalence is often better than the alternative. If our powers are not socially useful from the standpoint of those who could buy them or are less efficient than the social average, then we are unlikely to be or remain employed. The social force of the market serves as a sorting mechanism for our powers. It often determines which powers get shaped and reproduced in the first place.

Indeed, acknowledging that society is itself forceful adds a helpful element to SRT's philosophical anthropology. Up until this point, labor powers have been understood only as individual labor powers. Since society is itself a powerful force in shaping, actualizing, and constraining powers, space must be made for society and its forces not externally, as a mere add-on, but as a central part of SRT's view of what we are. By linking the "social" of SRT with the "labor powers" that are continuously produced and reproduced, we can develop SRT in a critical way.

Indeed, this philosophical anthropology has a strong critical force because it can help us identify some social arrangements as violent. SRT's account of human beings as essentially socially empowered also has the resources to condemn forms of social organization that are dominating, alienating, and disempowering. I've argued that what it means to be a human being is to be needy, active, socially situated, and capable of choosing amongst strategies for satisfying a rich set of needs. It follows that a social organization that ignores and reduces needs, forces some into inactivity, produces isolation, and needlessly constrains our ability to choose how to satisfy our needs can be considered a bad one.[18] A social organization is bad because it uses what we are to do violence to what we are.

This can all hang together because we do not simply *have* labor powers, but the continuous production and social reproduction of our powers makes them core parts of our very being. When Marx says that our labor power is the set of "mental and physical capabilities" that we use to produce something useful, he is referring not to some detachable extra that comes along with us, but instead to our mental and physical being itself. Marx called this our "embodied," "living personality."[19] That the reproduction of our labor powers makes them embodied parts of our lives is even clearer in *Capital*, when Marx writes: "The capital given in exchange for labor power is converted into necessaries, by the consumption of which the muscles, nerves, bones, and brains of existing laborers are reproduced, and new laborers are begotten." The powers we have to do useful things are non-detachable parts of our living embodiment and personality.[20] And even though these powers cannot exhaust the entirety of what we are, they necessarily make up a crucial part of each one of us.

Just how SRT can also critically appraise our social organization is not usually worked up in its specifics. For our purposes, it helps to center labor powers. To say that there is something deeply wrong about some organization of social force, it helps to have a deeper theory of what we are as socially situated capacities in our own right. The difference between thinking we *have* and thinking we *are* such capacities is, therefore, very significant. When we think of ourselves as needy, active, free, and socially empowering beings, then social forces that deny or constrain our capacities can be considered violences that harms us in our very being. If we are something that merely *has* labor powers in an external way, then this unknown deeper being that does the possessing might not be harmed when the capacities it simply holds are constrained.

To be harmed in one's possessions is a liberal position that defaults to protecting one's property. To be harmed as a capable living personality, however, motivates more radical commitments. On this view there is something deeply violent going on beyond the description that workers under conditions of capital have to sell their labor powers. As a commodity, these powers are transformed by activity from our "living personality" into the useful things our capacities can realize in the world. Yet we are not and did not sell these useful things—we in fact sold something more valuable by far. We sold our potentials to make these use-values. For instance, in *Capital* Marx writes: "The seller of labour-power, like the seller of any other commodity, realizes its exchange-value, and parts with its use-value. He cannot take the one without giving the other."[21] We accept a wage for making use-values, but only at the cost of alienating our potentials. In other words, we alienate a constitutive part of our living personality and in so doing constitute a foreign power that grows continuously stronger at our expense.

By centering labor powers in its view of what we are, SRT emphasizes that we are socially empowering beings. This is true even when our social organization fails to provide the best conditions for the development and free exercise of our capacities. Yet, capitalism's violence can never totally deny what we are. This is because we are always forming, using, or reproducing our labor powers even while subject to capitalism's domination. Thinking of the human as always in the process of developing, exercising, and reproducing powers is a bit awkward, but this active setup makes it easier to integrate the real, lived processes that shape our social relations in so many different ways.[22] It also finely stresses the living part of our "living personality."

Without a philosophical anthropology, it would be much harder to turn social descriptions into social criticisms. Someone could simply hold that even if our rich descriptions of constrained capacities were valid, it didn't follow from such descriptions that there was anything necessarily wrong. After all, someone might say, most of our potentials are constrained in some way. For descriptions of the social fact of constrained potentials to pass into a criticism that something is deeply harmful, there must be an at least implicit understanding of what we are as socially, needy, and varyingly empowering beings.

SRT has the resources to subject many different forms of social organizations to this deep criticism on the grounds that these organizations motivate structures, relations, and behaviors that limit our free, needy, socially self-empowering being. Put simply, since we are socially empowering beings, problematic social organization can be understood as those that inflict continuous damage on what we are.[23] One could even say they reproduce us as disempowered, contorted, and damaged beings.

LABOR POWER AND SOCIAL CRITICISM

The excerpt from Ana at the start of the chapter can help tether these points of theory back to the ground.[24] Ana herself has the ability to work and the ability to study. Setting her capacities to work provides Ana a wage and with it, much of what she needs. On the other hand, studying would produce another kind of useful thing—namely, an even more socially valuable set of labor powers that she could use to command a higher wage. But this is not all.

Ana also likes going to school and studying because she really enjoys learning itself, and learning computer programming in particular. She has a need to develop her capacities, as well as a need to work. But Ana is painfully aware that she is *not* as free to choose amongst her needs as she might be. She is not as free as she might be to enrich her living personality. She has family responsibilities, is without full legal standing or English as a first language, and owns no means of production. These all add up to making Ana depend on the exchange of her already existing labor powers in a competitive market. And she has to do so with some serious disadvantages.

Ana is socially disempowered by the overriding need to sell her labor power. She is then dominated by the labor market, in which that sale has to take place. Ana is then further constrained by the need to keep selling her labor power to produce use-values at others' command. This is incompatible with satisfying her other needs, like developing capacities for her own sake, or for improving her position in the labor market. Ana will be hard-pressed to find the resources to do more than reproduce her labor powers in something more than this disempowering and frustratingly constrained form. Ana is not alone in living through a society that stifles the free development of her powers. One that is set up to make her own values incompatible with those demanded by her bosses. A society that limits the powers that workers more generally can develop and actualize. It tends to limit labor powers to just those likely to be exchangeable for the wage required to reproduce them.

Given the just-developed view, a social reproduction theorist can say that Ana is being damaged, even dehumanized. The social organization of capitalism that Ana is immersed in reduces rather than enlarges the depths of her powers as a free, active, needy, and socially empowered being. Ana's family situation, status in the US, and language skills also limit the extent to which she can develop and exercise her labor powers. These factors lock Ana, more than some others, into a position that makes the activation of her labor powers hardly a matter of freely enriching her own personality. It is more one that straitjackets her powers to being actualized in ways that, at the same time, reproduce her own disempowerment.

When capital determines the contours of our social relations most of us are, at least in one sense, like Ana. We do not have direct access to the resources that we need to enrich our living personality, nor do we have the means we need to set our powers into profitable motion. We are forced to exchange whatever labor powers we find within our living personalities for a wage. This remains even if some are more fortunate than Ana, and the conditions for such exchange are less brutal and less dehumanizing. This is because the disempowering wage relation remains a dominant force in most of our lives. This violence is not unique to Ana because it is central to how capitalist societies produce use-values and reproduce labor powers. On this basis, SRT can take a critical stance: it can say that there is something not only quite bad about class-divided, capitalist societies, but something that requires they be transformed root and branch.

But we should not forget that there is something much more specific about the harm that Ana experiences. The constraint on her powers is not *only* due to the fact that she has to sell her labor powers for a wage. Ana's immigration status, language skills, and family situation played, for her, important roles in shaping the experience of her constraints. We would be missing a lot about the particular ways Ana's living personality is embodied and disempowered if we sidelined these aspects of her experience. It would not improve our insight if we insisted on only talking about the disconnected fact of labor powers sold for a wage. Ana's unique living personality is constrained via the wage relation she is forced to participate in. But this wage relation, while logically applicable across all capitalist societies, is constituted and experienced in tremendously different ways.[25]

As we have seen, labor power as an abstract idea applies trans-historically to all human beings. When approached as part of social analysis, however, we need to see just how labor powers are actually produced and reproduced in a given social context. And this is precisely what SRT does. SRT shows how capitalist societies are formed by capacities limited by citizenship status, language, and family situation. Of course that is not all—the list of socially disempowering influences can be expanded to include other constraining social dynamics like the processes underpinning racialization, misogyny, gender-binarism, ableism, religious persecution, and so much more.

SRT links the violence of these oppressive social logics to the labor powers that are produced, reproduced, and which must be sold under conditions of capital.[26] Capital's heartbeat of valorization requires the alienation of labor powers. Even though this is not the only form of violence, it is a powerful and dominating one. It demands that our living personalities fit the contorting paths by which capital valorizes. Since the ways our powers are made and sustained are dominated by capital, all the specific ways that making and sustaining happens can also be understood as part of capital's violence. And this is how SRT develops a social critique of capital alongside its logical analysis.

This social criticism of capital is valuable because capital is a social order, not just a system whose logic demands accumulation. When we understand the laws at the very heart of capital we definitely do so in a logical way. But *what* we are understanding logically is a thoroughly social process. The violence of capital is not inflicted on some social totality or on an abstract idea of labor powers—as if ideas themselves could be violated—it is to the embodied, living personalities in which so many labor powers reside. Capital does violence to actually living human beings.

For this reason, paying attention to stories like Ana's can help concretize our criticisms of the abstract logic of capital. Personal stories highlight the specific ways that powers are constrained and contorted. None of this precludes criticizing the logic of capital or capital as an overarching system, it merely specifies such criticism with attention to individual instances. After all, labor powers are not only commodities to be fit into the valorizing logic of capital. They are also the lived, embodied powers that while constrained like Ana's can be actualized and valued in many different ways.

From this vantage point we can see that SRT marks how social violence informs capital's need to valorize. It can do this without reducing every form and experience of social violence to a function of this valorization. Violent forms of oppression can shape living personalities and powers, even when labor powers are unsellable. These oppressions shape friend networks, family dynamics, and broader relations. This includes communities of support and resistance along with their hopes, conflicts, political views, institutions, and patterns of behavior. These social relationships and activities stem from our powers to do things we find useful. And the fact that some do not directly produce surplus-value does not change that fact. These and so many other social realities are not absolutely severed from the logic of capital. The key point is that few of their dynamics can be fully explained by the logic of capital alone.[27]

Social criticism of capital would point to what lies between and connects the violence in individual stories like Ana's and the larger social dynamics that encompass her. These include but are far broader than the violence of the wage, and the logic of valorization. Here, labor powers would need to be considered from the standpoint of the social histories that shape and contribute—but are not reducible to—the logic of capital. But this does not mean, as dual or multiple system theorists hold, that there are different systems with distinct logics. A body has abilities and needs that are distinct from (and not reducible to) the heart. This is true even though everything a body does is made possible by and in turn contributes to the beating rhythm of the heart. We need to sacrifice neither a view of the whole nor its foundational logic to recognize the specifics at play in parts.

SRT's social criticism of capital keys into this middle space, and builds bridges from individuals' experiences to their social conditions, and to the universal logic of capital. To do so, SRT proceeds in two distinct ways. The first path shows how social oppression is directly informed by the motions of capitalist exploitation. This approach highlights social relations of oppression that actually condition and reproduce the lived experience of exploitation or effective exclusion from the labor power market. These oppressions can be inaugurated by states, their institutions of social control, ideological apparatuses, the competition characteristic of capital itself, or all of these in tandem with others. The point of this approach is to show how social dynamics of oppression directly influence the circuits of valorization through which different kinds of labor powers are pushed to, or cannot, travel.

The second way SRT develops its social criticism of capital is by paying attention to social forces that have a more indirect influence on the paths labor powers follow in relation to capital. Anti-Black racism, for instance, is commonplace in the US and permeates the very fiber of social relations. People racialized as Black are disproportionately surveilled, grossly stereotyped in cultural presentation, and assumed to function as a singular political bloc. All this while living under so many signs and structures of white supremacy. Reading these aspects of racism solely from the vantage point of the valorization of capital, say as part of capital's drive to segment the working class, would be too simplistic, and miss far too much.

These forms of anti-Black racism have cumulative effects that structure the horizons of what looks useful. They influence which powers can be generated to which ends for everyone, not just those they affect most violently. Anti-Black racism is apparent also in hiring, loaning, housing, carceral, educational, and medical practices. These can be rather easily and directly tied to how people racialized as Black tend to be connected to the circuits of capital's valorization. But even these direct links also have socially significant effects that can be distinguished from their immediate connections to capital.

To appreciate anti-Black racism as a kind of broader social violence, SRT turns to its commitment to seeing our labor powers as part and parcel with our living personalities. It then shows how anti-Black racism is disempowering in its construction of social fears, aesthetic standards, assumptions about pain thresholds, and much else. Anti-Black racism is a source of so many needless, additional sources of stress, worry, and brutal violence. SRT can show how these forms of violence are produced and reproduced to both the detriment of Black people's potentials and in how those potentialities are permitted to or constrained from participating in capital's valorization processes.

Let's consider the implications of this. Systems and patterns of behavior that reproduce disempowering racialization can be appreciated for the specific and violent effects they have on living personalities. When social reproduction theorists hold that anti-Black racism is violent and oppressive, we are also making a damning social criticism of capital. This is because being racialized as Black in part shapes Black people's very embodiment and living personality. And this is true even before labor powers are brought to the market.[28] If the powers and potentials which capital requires workers bring to market are produced and reproduced by anti-Black racism, then capitalism is racist. This is true even though anti-Black racism is not reducible to or exclusively caused by capital's imperative to valorize.

Since labor powers sold and set in motion are absolutely essential to capital valorization, any social force that contorts our living personalities and does violence to our capacities can be included in what SRT criticizes when it criticizes capitalism. This violence plays out not in the abstract logic of capital, but in the actual powers that capital uses or shunts aside as it valorizes.[29] SRT's social criticism of capital is not only that it is violent and disempowering, but that it rests on violent, disempowering, and oppressive social relations as the paths for its valorization. These brutal relations are reproduced as necessarily as (because they are literally embodied in) the working class itself.

It is no accident then that racism's violent disempowerings are not only compatible with the logic of capital, but a key feature of how capitalism actually works. Racism is a social problem because in its many guises it is disempowering, while capital is a social problem because it draws on and reproduces disempowered living personalities. It is not that anti-Black racism is a direct and necessary result of the most abstract logic of capital, though anti-Black racism in the US is in large part the result of how the logic of capital was historically fleshed out. Racism today is a material force that specifies capital. It is one of the mediating social dynamics that ties the abstract logic of valorization to the lived, embodied experiences of millions.

Our labor powers can be appreciated as the socially specific and highly differentiated capacities we all have to produce a use-value of any description. These capacities are the minded and embodied potencies of our living personalities. When SRT sees these powers as multiple, capable of satisfying social needs, and in some sense freely directable, it has the background commitments needed to recognize capital's disempowering logic as a kind of social violence. The specific stories of such violence can then help us develop criticisms of race, gender, and so many other oppressive dynamics.

3

The Question of Immanence and the Social Form of Labor Power

And that's really why I joined the cooperative. I came, I learned about the concept of the cooperative and I liked it a lot. I've always worked in a group, so it seemed easy enough to collectivize the management with a group. In the cooperative, you don't feel alone anymore because, you know, when you work for an agency you do feel isolated, you feel … like there is a lot of responsibility on you personally. But the difference in a cooperative is that you feel like you have a lot of support, like there are people behind you who have your back. There are people behind you who care about the same things that you care about. You don't feel so alienated from things because you have to be honest. Like I said, I started because of necessity and in an agency people go primarily because of necessity, not because they love the work. Now I'm in the cooperative because I love the work, because I love to do it, because I feel good, because it gives me great personal satisfaction. And that's one of the most important things in life. And economically, you feel good that your work has more value. (Alicia, on how relations of production influence labour conditions and practice)[1]

Alicia shows us that the organization of powers matters in a deeply personal way. When working for a private agency the organization of her capacities was deeply alienating, while in the workers' cooperative, the organization was affirming and supportive. This distinction provides an opportunity to show how and why Social Reproduction Theory need not be committed to celebrating any and all powers. Alicia also shows that what counts as a freer power and what counts as a constrained power is socially situated. This bears directly on how SRT thinks through its normative commitments, and how it construes the relation between "ability" and "disability."

The social criticism of capital developed in the last chapter leaned heavily on unpacking what Marx meant by "labour-power." I showed that SRT centers our capacities as a key part of its philosophical anthropology. That is, as a key part of what we are as human beings. This approach can be fleshed out by examining the embodied labor powers that form our living personalities in so many different ways. Through diverse powers in the midst of constraint, SRT transforms recognition of the specific ways our living personalities are constrained into social criticisms of capital. SRT is committed to valuing the diverse powers embodied in living personalities as ways we can affirm rather than do violence against our very being. It focuses on these capacities over and against the social paths and logic of capital that produce and sustain a violent, dehumanizing regime of value.

Our diverse labor powers provide the tools to think not only that things are bad now, but that they could be organized in other, better ways. The tremendous diversity of our powers means they can never be fully represented in any actual activity. Nor are they fully encompassed by any given set of institutions. Our potentials, in other words, are far broader than how we set them in motion.

This freedom to do and be otherwise means that even when constrained, we have the ability to choose amongst our different powers. We can also choose different ways of activating the same powers. In the quote that begins this chapter Alicia, who works mostly with the elderly as a home health-care aid, describes how her relationship to work changed. Having worked for a private agency, she instead joined a workers' cooperative. The same capacities Alicia used while working for the agency are being set in motion, but the cooperative relations that set them in motion now make a tremendous difference for Alicia.

Even when highly curtailed, this points to an element of freedom for Alicia, and for all of us. And it might go without saying, but exercising this freedom makes us feel good. For Marx, this love of our own freedom, and then what flows from it, is a deep part of every living personality. We often pursue social relations that enable the freedom to self-determine as an important goal in itself—we feel constrained when an external, dominating force we don't have a say in directing controls our potentials or dictates our actions. As Alicia put it after changing to the cooperative, "I love the work, because I love to do it, because I feel good, because it gives me great personal satisfaction." It is not only the case that we have some space to choose which needs we wish to satisfy and how we wish to satisfy them, as Alicia highlights, enlarging that space is itself a good thing. The freedom to actively self-determine is an essential—and valuable—feature of what it means for beings like us to set our powers into motion.

This freedom can be exercised in unlimited ways. Some of the activities we freely pursue require "close attention," and a "process [which] demands that, during the whole operation, the workman's will be steadily in consonance with his purpose." Or, we may pursue a less demanding activity merely because it "gives play to ... bodily and mental powers."[2] We can be actively free in both strict attention to a precise and demanding process, as well as the unruly, rambunctious, unrestrained, and joyous exercise of our powers beyond rules. Whether in deep concentration or in a playful release from strict rules, we exercise and have evidence of our freedom.

The scope of our freedom can be wider or narrower, depending on the constraints imposed by our enveloping social relations.[3] As Alicia's narrative shows us, even when performing the same kind of work, we might operate under strikingly different circumstances. The unfolding production, actualization, and reproduction of our powers in more or less free forms is, as we saw, the very core of what SRT studies. To follow Alicia's lead, we can value how workers' control makes workers feel less "alienated." Cooperative self-determination tokens a different, freer way of valuing work.[4] Freer powers are therefore also the centerpiece of SRT's critical strategy. SRT is justified in making labor power such a central part of its commitments because powers to actively satisfy needs are the real basis of any social organization in the first place. Without them we would all languish in our individual inactivity. In a short amount of time we would simply perish from unmet need.

Like all concepts that can help develop criticism of capital, theorists need to focus on what it would take to flesh out abstract concepts with content, and perhaps even more importantly, center the ugly realities that abstractions too often sweep under the rug. As shown at the end of the last chapter, it would not be enough to simply say that capital requires the sale of free labor powers for a wage. While no doubt true, what our capacities look like when set in motion requires more. We have to trace them back not to wage-labor that appears homogeneous due to abstraction, but to the potentialities of different living bodies and personalities, which Marx insisted was their basis. Developing the critical thrust of this idea, Marx held that capital does create abstract and homogeneous labor: capital's "general value form is the reduction of all kinds of actual labour to their common character of being human labour generally, of being the expenditure of human labour power." Marx's point here is that capital relies on and reproduces a tremendous and growing amount of specific capacities to labor while determining their *value* in an abstract, one-size-fits-all way.[5]

Between the universal logic of capital and the individual, living personality, theorists of social reproduction like Martha Gimenez trace the social forces that pressure people and the ways labor powers are set in motion.[6] These forces condition how our powers are produced in the first place, what they are actively shaped into, and how social relations constrain or free our powers in their exercise. Social forces impact how our powers are reproduced in the broadest sense—individually and socially as well as day to day and inter-generationally. In this way, freedom can be moved from the broad brush stroke of an abstract truth to increasingly fine-grained social determinations. We can track how the scope of freedom available to us is realized only in light of the constraints that condition our capacities.[7] Every individual has their powers formed, rendered actualizable, and reproduced through their relation to evolving social forces.[8] After all, social forces do not spring on us out of the blue— they take their specific shape from the combined results of how we have already navigated the ways they pressure us in different ways.

This attention to labor powers, social forces, and living personalities means that theorists can criticize disempowering social forces like mindless productivism, ableism, and transphobia as constraints on our own capacities. That is, they are understood as forms of violence against the powers that are essential parts of what we are. Like Alicia, SRT is optimistic that our powers can be formed and valued in less alienating and more fulfilling ways. Even when we are constrained by capital and find it difficult to organize and resist, it is always in principle possible to challenge rather than conserve, or stabilize, the violent domination of capital.

This emphasis on freedom is precisely why social reproduction theorists tend to reject so many automatic responses. SRT has little time for the strictly linear potency of unavoidable reflexes—whether the power to kick forward in a doctor's knee-jerk reflex test or the unavoidable proletariat revolution theorized by too many mechanistic versions of Marxism. It presents powers not as fated to their specific actualization, but as possibilities that are actualized in ways that are far less free than could be the case.

An emphasis on freedom and labor powers comes with possible risks. How, for example, can we value some of our powers over others? This problem can only be avoided if SRT develops the resources to make different value judgments. Another risk revolves around the notion of "power" itself, which can be construed in terms that are ableist and ultimately disempowering. In what follows, then, I explore the nature of these problems and develop solutions that, when synthesized, build a more robust version of SRT.

WHICH KINDS OF POWERS?

How can we transform SRT's commitment to the freedom of labor powers into something more valuable and nuanced than a banal and ultimately liberal approach. We can't stop short at equally valuing all individual freedoms, nor the free realization of any and all labor powers. If all labor powers set into motion contribute in their own way to reproducing a social totality, what then can justify valuing the free exercise of some capacities over the free exercise of others? And if some capacities can only be actualized in violent ways, what resources does SRT have to condemn them? Some might worry that SRT's commitment to empowering labor is so broad that it cannot differentiate beneficial from harmful uses of powers, or that it cannot differentiate between better or worse powers themselves.

Let's look at Alicia's story as an example. One might wonder how SRT could value forms of workers' control, realized in miniature in enterprises like Alicia's cooperative, more than the work done by a manager at the private agency she left? Or, in a different vein, can the theory value the work of geologists working to spread knowledge about the likelihood and physical effects of global climate change over and against the work done by geologists working for extractive industries? In both examples similar capacities are set in motion—management and geological research. A theory that simply values all labor powers as equivalent will fail to make necessary distinctions between them.

The problem becomes more difficult when we think about how different powers are set to different ends. A theory which flatly values the free empowerment of capacities would have difficulty holding that the power to care for the infirm is better than the kinds of powers that make lives harder. It could not, for instance, tell caring for the elderly from taking carbon out of the ground and preparing it to be consumed as energy. The capacity to care for those in need and the capacity to extract carbon for energy would be just different species of labor power. If all SRT can do is promote the freedom of labor powers, it would be hard to say that any capacity ought to be preferred over any other.

A solution to this seeming impasse lies in the way SRT situates labor power. Others have pointed to the specific ways that the realization of some labor powers would, in their effects, constrain the free use of others. If the freedom of labor powers is considered in light of the effects that stem from their actualization, then valuing some powers over others presents little difficulty. The social conditions that would maximize our freedom to actively satisfy needs would be preferred over those that constrain the scope of our freedom. For example, it is better to work cooperatively than for a private agency because the cooperative use of labor powers contributes to the empowerment of oneself and others. In the private enterprise, however, labor powers are exploited by the private bosses and managers. They use their return on investment not just to maintain their domination but to grow capital and thereby further restrain the scope of workers' freedom.

Since care work normally develops or reproduces our powers, SRT values the many kinds of care work over the many kinds of carbon-extractive work. In one sense, it is no doubt true that the energy provided by carbon extraction develops our powers. But as we've known for a while, carbon extraction is responsible for global warming and its devastating effects. Through the burning of fossil fuels required first to extract the carbon, then to transport and refine it, and finally to use the result for energy or as an ingredient in industrial production, extractive powers can only be set in motion in ways that harm the conditions we need to reproduce our powers. Even worse, the warming effects of producing and relying on carbon exacerbates social oppressions in myriad ways.

There will always be some grey, murky areas when trying to make comparative judgments about labor powers. For instance, assuming one had to choose between the two, there might be reasonable debate between social reproduction theorists about whether it is more valuable to organize social pressure to transition to renewable energies or to defend communities against the rare-earth mining required for a transition from carbon dependence. There can be no clearly correct answer given the level of abstraction with which the question is posed. Answering it with a social reproduction lens would require much more detailed information about the specific conditions and likely results of each possible path. But we do not need to lose the forest for the trees. We do not need to be climate scientists to know that some labor powers need to be radically restrained if we are to live on this planet and with social relations that enable our freedom.

If restraining some powers is a condition for the development or even continued existence of others, then SRT has a helpful response to the worry that anything goes so long as it's some kind of labor power. Taken together, this means that SRT does not involve itself in a contradiction: holding that our living personalities should be empowered also means that some of our potentialities should not be actualized. By moving from the abstract to the specifics of social place and likely effects over time, SRT privileges powers that set into motion chains of increasing freedom over and against the constraining dynamics of others.

As a result of its concerns with production and the economy, Marxism has always had a difficult relationship with productivism. Productivism is a tendency to value production above all else. It can make the mistake of believing that the more we produce, the more we realize something essential about ourselves.[9] Yet, SRT requires that some forms of production, like the ability to exploit labor powers for a profit, and some specific abilities, like the ability to burn the planet into uninhabitability, should not be actualized. Further, the power not to work, to withhold labor through striking is an essential part of our freedom. After all, if we had no freedom to determine when to actualize our powers, we would be exactly like automatic machines. The freedom to direct our powers must also be our freedom to restrain them.

THE QUESTION OF "DISABILITY" AND THE FORMS OF POWER

The second problem that SRT would do well to avoid is the pitfall of ableism. Ableism is far too often an unreflective part of theories that value maximizing our powers. The stress on power, capacity, even potency at the root of SRT's values and judgments may indeed give some reason to pause. There must be a response to any mode of thinking that conflates valuing workers' powers with the violent normalizations that render those with less or different powers value*less*.

If SRT has a deep-rooted commitment to labor power, what can it offer to disabled people? From this view, we can identify disabled people as those who through "disability" are *dis*empowered and marginalized if not excluded from acting to satisfy their own and social needs.[10] But how can SRT take a critical stance not only against some powers, but the larger social conditions that exclude, disempower, or fail to recognize the potentialities of so many in the first place?

A response to these important questions cannot take the same approach as the power-withholding or strike-based response to the worry about productivism. For those who have socially diminished or unrecognized powers to satisfy needs, using one's powers to *not* work does not hold the same promise as it does for those whose powers are more fully confirmed by society. The radical power to withhold work is not, in other words, held in the same way by everyone. Those who are embodied and immersed in social relations that reduce their ability to wield this radical weapon will find little comfort in a theory that promotes the labor powers they have a harder time exercising in the first place. Put simply: there are those who can more easily work and threaten to strike, and those who have a harder time doing so.

People without officially recognized work often do support strikes in myriad ways. Joining strikers on picket lines, disrupting the flow of commerce, physically occupying strategic locations, taking care of strikers' emotional, physical, and cultural needs, encouraging others' active solidarity, preserving and sharing the history of radical struggles, and building deeper community support for strikes are all valuable, and often indispensable to a strike's success. That "disabled" people often engage in such solidarizing acts should throw into question the standards we use to distinguish "disability." It makes clear that "disability" is always determined from a certain social judgment regarding which of our powers are most worth actualizing. In capitalist societies, capital's demand for maximum profitability determines who can perform officially recognized work, and who not. This division largely sets up who is "able-bodied" and who falls on the other side of that line.

When SRT values the freedom of labor powers, however, it is committed to a rich plurality of capacities even when capitalist social relations force them to take the form of constrained or unrealized potentials. This foundational commitment also informs SRT's relation to the very legitimate worry about ableism.[11] SRT challenges the ways in which our rich diversity of capacities are limited by ableist framings and social conditions. In particular, SRT can center the social conditions that make it harder for people with different abilities or impairments to join a workforce.[12] SRT is then far less interested in determining the proportion of our uniqueness that can be shown to rest exclusively on natural causes.

This is because in nearly every single instance, our capacities are affirmed or denied and reproduced not naturally, but socially.

The incompatibility of many disabled people with conventional work-sites or their consignment to the least rewarded parts of contemporary workforces have a range of "knock-on" impacts. They create dynamics of dependence which are ripe for increased risk, discrimination, and many different forms of abuse. The resulting psychological and physical tolls are all but unlimited. They are then compounded by the fact that disabil-ities are also often registered and formally assessed by the state, obliging people to go through an often degrading process of convincing govern-ments that they are sufficiently disadvantaged to receive support. This is, of course, a draining and highly stress-inducing process in itself.

Every time any living personality is systematically prevented from realizing their powers, this exclusion re-entrenches a social norm about what is configured under the rubric of disability. This socially con-structed oppression can become self-fulfilling in two ways. First, when labor powers are marginalized or ignored, they are left untapped and constrained to remain mere potentials. Preventing powers from being actualized is itself a disabling dynamic. Quite literally, such sidelining prevents powers from being confirmed through use and reproduction. Second, sidelining powers in this way re-entrenches the social percep-tion of what counts as an ability or power in the first place, and what, on the other side, counts as a kind of disability. The effects of ableist social forces are therefore self-reproducing in practical and ideological ways that tend to hide their violence in especially pernicious ways.

SRT avoids the tendency to pathologize some as more or less powerful than others, by refusing to center individual circumstances in isolation from social context. SRT directs our focus on the ways social dynamics organize the chances that powers can be developed and actualized. It refuses to accept existing determinations of what is considered an ability, even when such determinations claim or appear to be "natural." Many disabled people play central roles in the reproduction of society, even if how their impairments are treated socially might restrict them from finding steady or formally recognized work.

In his *Critique of the Gotha Voting Program* Marx demands "from each according to his ability," only *after* overcoming bourgeois constraints on how abilities themselves are socially developed.[13] Indeed, in the same text, Marx called any approach that would instead focus on returning to workers just what they can produce given *existing* social determination of their powers "obsolete verbal rubbish."[14] For Marx, the foremost concern was changing the social relations that determine what people can do. Attempts to organize distribution of resources on "unequal individual endowment and thus productive capacity" were entirely insufficient.[15] In stressing how social relations shape the very form of what counts as a capacity, and whether or not it can be put to use, SRT extends Marx's valuable insight into a powerful response to ableism. The normative commitment to labor power provides not just another ableist framework, but a robust critique of social forces that institutionalize and normalize disempowering ableisms.

SRT's approach to disability does not proclaim a universal equality of capacities. It starts by acknowledging our differences, and then reveals the need to appreciate how the differentiating violence of capitalist social relations develops those differences in highly limiting ways. As the long-running children's public television program *Mr. Rogers* was fond of saying, "some can do some things, and some can do others." SRT does not pass judgment on what individuals can or cannot do. In many cases, that would be a form of useless moralism. As a social theory, SRT explores how abilities are formed and then socially shaped such that the source of its criticisms is more social than moral. As a theory with deeply held values, it demands the largest possible freedom to develop, use, and reproduce labor powers for all of our different living personalities.

This kind of freedom requires that our labor powers take a radically different form. Our potential capacities range far beyond the constraints that give them shape today. How we value labor powers and the very forms that they take as "able" or not can be explored and thrown into question. We can broaden Amy De'ath's call to explore the social reproduction of gender and gendered labor through the value-form into a call to explore and criticize the socially disempowering ways all labor powers are formed by capital's violent regime of value.[16]

Our relative labor powers are all constrained to take the form of something equivalent to—and therefore exchangeable with—the value expressed in a wage. This socially powerful force prevents our specific, differently capable living personalities from constituting values in the exercise of our freedom. The oppression of "disability" in particular helps highlight the formative violence inflicted on living personalities. In capitalist contexts, we are reduced to or, even worse, excluded from the way our powers are confirmed as valuable in their own right by the given form values as labor powers are constrained to take.

When SRT makes the locus of its theorizing the freedom of labor power, it sees the current organization and scope of powers as reproducing a given social regime of dividing ability from disability. It then throws this regime in its entirety into question. Recognizing social constraints on need-satisfying power also means recognizing that the very form and constitution of powers hangs on one's social context. If capital's expansion enlarges the scope and changes the relations, forms, needs, and value of labor power, then the history of capital itself gives the lie to supposed "natural" determinations of ability. This recognition prompts hope for a totally new set of demarcations: less disabling for those with impairments, and allowing a broadening horizon of human potentials to be socially realized and valued.

Radically different, non-capitalist relations would not merely create different paths for the production and reproduction of our powers. They would fundamentally alter the very form they take. In miniature and certainly incomplete form, Alicia's experience of moving from a private agency to a cooperative already suggests something quite similar. Alicia moved from working out of compulsion, to working in a way that at least partially expresses her freedom: "I started because of necessity and in an agency people go primarily because of necessity, not because they love the work. Now I'm in the cooperative because I love the work, because I love to do it, because I feel good, because it gives me great personal satisfaction." And consider the difference between Alicia's former isolation and her current sense of social-belonging: "In the cooperative, you don't feel alone anymore because, you know, when you work for an agency you do feel isolated." Finally, it is remarkable how Alicia's power moved from a false representation of her living personality to a more consistent one. As she puts it: "the difference in a cooperative is that you feel like you have a lot of support, like there are people behind you who have your back. There are people behind you who care about the same things that you care about. You don't feel so alienated from things because you have to be honest."

In and of themselves workers' cooperatives are not revolutions against capital. Since cooperatives today are forced to compete with private businesses, they tragically tend to reproduce relations and forms of labor they were developed to serve as a bulwarks against. Still, even this partial transformation gives us a glimpse of more thoroughgoing improvements we can work towards. Beyond simply feeling better about the work, the form that Alicia's powers took became social, less alienated, and for that reason more an expression of her freedom. This is probably what led Alicia to feel so palpably better about the cooperative mode of organizing work. Since Alicia's experience largely flows not from some personal idiosyncrasy, but from the structure of cooperation itself, it provides a glimpse of the possibilities for revolutionizing labor powers. A revolutionary reorganization would make it possible to have labor powers organized in a self-empowering rather than alienating way. Accomplishing this would effect a major change for the better in all of our living personalities.

4

The Body and Gender in
Social Reproduction Theory

People who were too young and too naughty for the ball scene so you could go to a Kiki or Kiki function and it was less shady no body gets chopped you're not walking for money none of the girls have their titties yet or any surg (surgery) so you don't feel shamed for not having work done, it was just less at stake, there's no predatory behavior by older people who prey on kids which is a thing sorry ballroom community do better, so yeah that was why the Kiki balls were a lot of fun … Showing off, being fab, having your friends there, cheering you on, being in competition, winning if you can win. And then afterwards people, putting their money together to go to the diner and get food, taking everybody or taking over the diner, people like gagging, were like all these horrendously queer kids, oh my god, if anybody saw us, I guess they would be so disturbed. (Alyssa Pariah, on gender affirming Kiki functions)[1]

Attending to our labor powers showed that we have the ability to produce them in very different forms. But while recognizing that powers and "ability" are socially produced and reproduced, some perhaps wonder just how deep socially reproductive powers go. Do they include the processes of gendering beyond biology? As Alyssa shows us, merely naturalistic conceptions of the body and gender would not be able to appreciate trans people's self-engendering powers. Yet some prior versions of Social Reproduction Theory are indeed premised on these problematic assumptions. I then suggest that SRT's analysis of oppression as well as its liberatory horizon is better pursued by replacing naturalisms with an even more thoroughgoing account of the body, its capacities, and gender as socially produced and reproduced.

The worry in the previous chapter, that valuing the freedom of labor powers as such prevented making critical differences between them, was met by determining labor powers in light of their unfolding effects.

Paying attention to the unfolding consequences of powers when they are set into motion helped show how SRT can be committed to freedom in a nuanced way. Freedom is not simply a universal fact, it describes how our capacities can be or are restrained from being actualized.

The second worry, that SRT's emphasis on capacities falls into a dangerous ableism, was met by bringing disability into clearer view. Being disabled is not a natural condition—what counts as a power or ability, and therefore also what does not, is grounded less in biological facts than in the form our living personalities are constrained to take in order to be considered valuable within capitalist societies. SRT then explores and challenges the forms that determine our living personalities in constraining ways.

A third worry, and the subject of this chapter, is voiced by Alyssa. For Alyssa, Kiki functions provide the space to be comfortably, even joyously embodied because they affirmed her gender. But outside Kiki functions, things are different. In the diners after Kiki balls Alyssa remembers being worried about people gagging, and being disturbed at the presence of a group of queer kids. This reaction is often due to assumptions about the "natural" way bodies should be and express their gender. And this naturalism lends itself to the strength of gender oppression. Even some prior articulations of SRT have taken naturalistic paths when thinking the body and its gendered existence. Yet, there is no need to continue doing so. In fact, some of SRT's primary commitments, as I'll show, motivate against different naturalisms. A response to the third worry then grounds SRT in the freedom we have to configure ourselves beyond naturalistic constraints.

Taken together—freedom situated through material consequences, form-determined constraints, and the liberatory potential of our powers, can add up to a hard core of SRT's grounding in labor powers. The first without the other two would at best offer a social history. It would always fall short of providing us with an actionable way forward. The second without the first has developed into debates too far removed from the social history needed to shed light on specific forms of oppression. It has also, without the third, sometimes taken a too pessimistic view of our fate. Finally, the third without the other two would be just another shallow call to pull ourselves up by our bootstraps. Yet taken together, the three parts of SRT's grounding serve radical ends.

Here, I synthesize the material consequences, form-determined constraints, and the liberatory potential of our powers by exploring two earlier approaches to social reproduction that *do* take some naturalistic routes. I have in mind Silvia Federici's and then Lise Vogel's accounts of SRT. These paths risk pushing SRT into some gender-essentialist commitments that potentially sideline queer people, and result in poorly construing the living personalities at the basis of everyone's labor powers.

Both Federici and Vogel offer valuable challenges to narrow value-productive lenses by working through the relations that set sexed processes of valorization on their paths. So, the goal in what follows is not so much to criticize Federici or Vogel themselves. The goal is rather to push the structure of their positions at particular points in a way that can be more queer than they have been in the past. In particular, while trans-inclusive analysis was previously not a pressing concern for many feminist theories, today not addressing these concerns is inexcusable. Despite the debt leftists concerned with theorizing women's oppression owe Federici and Vogel in particular, it is important to mark where their assumptions and approaches can be improved on. Though we should seek to improve on theoretical origins, it should be abundantly clear that so much of what makes SRT a robust theory is the way it draws on and extends the radical history of these Marxist feminists.

Still, Federici's early focus on the female body as the recurring locus of primitive accumulation marked female-sexed bodies as a, if not *the*, key source for capital accumulation. The body is, without doubt, central for any materialist notion of capacities, history, or social theory. But, the naturalized body present in Federici is often a primitive resource and a bald fact. This is—even if not intentional—a deeply conservative commitment. Vogel, for her part, offers a more compelling political economy than Federici. Vogel also links the biological capacity of gestation to disadvantages in capitalist social arrangements. But she still relies on just and only that political economy and biology to think the category "woman" and thereby also women's oppression. Both can be improved upon.

SILVIA FEDERICI: GENDER IN *CALIBAN AND THE WITCH*

Following Federici, in *Caliban and the Witch*, we are shown how—from rapes to witch-hunts—bodies were turned into labor powers by nascent capitalist demands for regular, uninterrupted profits. For capital to accomplish that transformative goal "the body had to die so labor power could live."[2] Federici's idea that prior to early capitalist developments the body had to die to make room for labor power suggests that there was a stable, clear, natural, pre-capitalist body that was violated. The pre-rational, magical conception of the body had to be killed. Capital required that this kind of body be replaced with a form of subjectivity appropriate to the demystified industry of more regularized value extraction.

This is an ahistorical and naturalistic account of the body that is only partially complicated by the historical story of the revolutions brought about in the emergence of capital. It is an essential commitment and key feature of Federici's social philosophy. It stands even or precisely when she recognizes the changed, contorted, abused, and resistant bodies produced and reproduced today. For Federici, there are large-scale demographic forces like the black plague, but not much of a relational conception of embodied subjects, much less of history. She tends to rely on and value the force of diversely realizable and resistant embodiments prior to capital which are oddly not contorted by pre-capitalist forms of domination. The witch and her sometimes violent, proud, and tragically quashed resistance against the constraint of a narrowly rationalizing social order is the very starting point for Federici's account of capitalist social reproduction.

The way bodies had been produced, reproduced, symbolically conceived, socially acknowledged, related in and through a social order, and the many ways they were put to work or excluded from satisfying needs nearly all fall by the wayside. Instead, Federici offers an account of the body as such which, as such, undergoes or fights some violent change. This primacy of the body is therefore what I'll call an ontological commitment. Federici's social reproduction is committed to an ontology of natural bodies, rather than to a situated and relational determination of bodies. Bodies tend to be sexed naturalistically, and are only gendered in two extreme ways. Either through liberatory and sexed resistance on one side or the violently sexed re-formation of bodies to fit the emerging needs of capital on the other. In this way, bodies are gendered, but they don't seem to do much gendering through relational practice with each other.

Capital, for Federici, therefore imposes an exogenous shock on women's bodies. The impact is such that the site of resistance and repression is then the bare but sexed body as well. But on this view, it is hard to see what prompted the movement towards what Federici calls the Cartesian constructions of the body. Federici argues that such bodies are mere bodies distinct from and controlled by mind, but it is unclear what happened to make this bifurcation acceptable let alone plausible as a nascent view. Is it because the structure of a body split from mind keys into the structure of capital's disciplinary demands? Or is the split structure an ever-present, underlying possibility waiting for the violence required to bring it to light?

Federici either assumes, against her romantic pre-capitalist story, some constant version of capital's push towards rationalizing more diffuse notions of embodiment. In this way, the Cartesian form of embodiment would be naturally selected for at some point. Or she can avoid this ahistorical assumption of constant capitalist pressures. In that case, there is only the inexplicable violence of an exogenous shock not itself prepared for by the very bodies it comes to dominate. In other words, capital inexplicably emerges to do its disciplinary violence on natural bodies or bodies are always potentially ripe for capitalist domination. Either the inevitability of a seamless fit or the impossibility of a social reproduction explanation of new and newly violent gender relations. In both instances, there is no history of the relations of production including, in particular, how our sexed and gendered bodies are subject to the domination we also play some role in reproducing.

Federici describes the move to capitalism in the following way:

> not only did the [proletariat] body lose all naturalistic connotations, but a body-function began to emerge, in the sense that the body became a purely relational term, no longer signaling any specific reality, but identifying instead any impediment to the domination of Reason. This means that the whole proletariat became a body ... in particular the weak, irrational female.[3]

Federici's ontological commitment is clear: a relational determination of what bodies do is an advent of capitalist ideology, not a methodological premise for history as such.

For Federici, the reduction of bodies to relational determination is a problem, and not a gift or an analytic resource for thinking through and challenging oppressive logics. The female is developed as the logical conclusion of this relational body. And this relational determination of female bodies is problematic—rather than emancipatory—for Federici precisely because the body is no longer a natural reality. Federici sees this as a problem crafted by capital and its Cartesian notions of the body.

But given Federici's naturalistic ontology, the solution can never be relying on the powers fostered by relational determinations. It is therefore hard to see political possibilities for transcending existing constraints.[4] When holding that capital robs women of diverse natural powers by constraining women to the social reproduction of labor power for capital, the solution for Federici is *not* a revolution beyond capitalist modes of social reproduction. Instead she tends to offer an upper limit of recommoning, renaturalization, and a return to resistance instead of revolution.[5]

The emphasis on the natural body as diversely realizable and opposed to violently narrow constraints of capital may seem to hold promise for a queer approach. Still, one might wonder what kind of SRT can flow from such a view of bodies? The answer is one that has a tendency to double-down on the value of bodies preferred for their mere fact of persisting despite being under threat. Such bodies are in the mode of resistance, to be sure. But for resistance construed naturalistically there will be negative consequences in general, and for queer people in particular.

Naturalist notions of embodiment may promote freer, non-reproductive sexual relations as well as many different family relations, but they will not have as much to offer trans men and women, or non-binary ways of being a gendered body.[6] Nor will they be able to consider the relational fluidity of gender in both its social determinations nor in the ways individuals varyingly experience and reproduce our gender over the course of our evolving social conditions. This criticism of capital's construction of the body as female, relational, and irrational, misses the way all bodies can be put into relational practice *beyond* naturalistic limits. In other words, this approach overlooks the gendered body as a possible sight of self-determination.

The space we have to navigate gender freedom, though far from complete, again tokens one aspect of a wider liberatory potential. Our desires and powers to navigate how our body is socially gendered draw from oppressive regimes, but these self-engendering capacities also demonstrate our ability to set new dynamics into motion over and against restraining ones. Because this is both an individual power, and in many senses a highly socially curtailed one, our ability to be and express our bodies more freely means the category of gender is best conceived through challengeable social, and not natural, determinations.

Alyssa's description of her experience with the Kiki balls finely illustrates this gender freedom. For Alyssa, Kiki balls provided a competitive but safe place for trans individuals to express gender in completely free and freeing ways. The supportive social setting and the personal, competitive, and performative aspect of self-gendering all work together. Being able to show off without shame and receive social recognition is then put in stark relief by the way Alyssa pictures people at the diner gagging and being disturbed by "horrendously" non-normative gender expressions. The Kiki balls provide a space for socially affirming gender, but they exist within a larger world which includes social disgust at gender queer individuals.

The powers we have to navigate between social constraints and individual desires regarding gender are important parts of our living personality. After all, at least today, there is little space to not be gendered. In this light, the category "woman" is better conceived not as a kind of body that suffers and resists through an already-present, natural set of capacities, but as a socially delimited way of living, working, desiring, and being a socially recognized living personality. Like any kind of living personality, all women are both variably empowered and limited in their potencies.[7]

With this notion of "woman," SRT can chart the misogynistic ways gender is socially produced in coercive and constraining ways for all women. But it also leaves room for noticing the limitations on trans women's potentialities.[8] Alyssa mentions surgery, which in the US is always subject to one's ability to pay, as well as walking for money, that is, doing sex work, which comes with its own risks and difficulties for trans women. This is why building communities and spaces like Kiki balls is so important. They affirm and grow gender freedom.

In the hands of Noah Zazanis, Jules Gleeson, and Michelle O'Brien a social reproduction approach to studying the communities that help empower individuals in their relation to gender is already being done at a high level.[9] Once gender is appreciated as a way of being that we make—though of course not under conditions of our own choosing—SRT moves from configuring gender as a natural site of resistance to gender as a socially determined site of powers or potentials. Not taking this path and sticking with a more naturalistic reading presents significant risks.

Even when following accounts like Federici's in which "woman" is considered plural, wide-ranging in its possible determinations, and an expression of freedom that is violated by the force of capitalism, gender remains needlessly bounded. Those who challenge the stability or bounds of the supposedly natural category are beyond its scope. The specific harms suffered by transitioning, gender fluid and non-binary people are then unthematizable. This version of SRT would amount to another theoretical marginalization that leaves behind the already vulnerable. While Federici herself never makes these moves, it is a pitfall that her theoretical strategy remains open to.

One alternative to such a strategy is to try to multiply natural categories. Perhaps fluid, trans, and non-binary genders are similarly "natural" such that, much like "woman," further categories can name people who have always responded, and are still responding, to capital's violence. While gender has never been a rigid binary, what it means to be trans, fluid, or non-binary was never naturally determined. Indeed, multiplying natures does not help appreciate the historically changing compositions, organizations, strategies, sites, and goals of anti-capitalist struggle.

Reducing people to naturalistic determinations of gendered bodies arrayed against capital's violence does little to mark the specific ways capital constrains differing living personalities from developing and using their powers. The diminished power of a cis woman to rely on communal medical practices is quite different, for instance, from the diminished power of a trans woman to access the surgeries or hormone therapies she may need to more freely embody and express her gender. The natural potential some cis women, trans men, and non-binary people have to gestate must be understood not only as a natural fact, but in light of how misogynistic and gender-normative social dynamics enable or constrain access to the support anyone needs when becoming pregnant, gestating, and giving birth.

Put more simply, SRT can choose between resistance as a defense of our bodily natures or a model of labor powers that sees our living personalities as capable of evolving far beyond any notion of what they were, should, or even could be. The difference is between preserving what we are through resistance and empowering us to freely create what we wish to be.

LISE VOGEL: GENDER AND GENDER OPPRESSION IN
MARXISM AND THE OPPRESSION OF WOMEN

In *Marxism and the Oppression of Women*, Lise Vogel holds that "women's oppression in class-societies is rooted in women's differential position with respect to generational replacement-processes," and she refers to women's role "as child-bearer, child-rearer" of sexually binary replacement laborers.[10] Vogel also tends to view women's biology in a naturalist way, yet this naturalism is in one sense more open than Federici's, while potentially less open in another. On one side, the consequences of Vogel's natural bodies are socially determined. The natural facts of biology only become sources of oppression given certain enveloping social conditions. And this allows for a sharper criticism of capitalism. On the other, however, this naturalism roots women's oppression in biology and, in so doing, risks leaving under-developed other sources for women's gender oppression as well as gender oppressions other than women's.

So where Federici's naturalism prompts a theory of social reproduction that can privilege a range of "natural," resistant bodies over and against their unnatural constraint to reproducing labor powers for capital, Vogel's "differential position" provides a clearer, relational determination. Vogel writes, "the left wing of the socialist movement ... accorded with the general premises of the social-reproduction perspective ... reject the universal categories of 'woman' or 'the family' as theoretical starting points. Instead each focuses on the specificity of women's oppression in different classes in a given mode of production."[11] Vogel recognizes that in capitalist modes of production women disproportionately bear the burden of inter-generational reproduction. For this reason, women are at a disadvantage in labor markets.

This is undoubtedly true, as most people who gestate and then care for newborn infants are indeed women. Many women indeed have reproductive capacities, and these powers are indeed biological and embodied in obvious ways. Carrying a fetus to term is an embodied power that can be, and for some surrogates in fact is, a kind of work.[12] And this gestational work is not easy—making a baby is often nauseating, exhausting, painful, even dangerous work. Further, in the course of pregnancy, other capacities are often highly constrained. Especially where contraception is not widely available, even the risk of pregnancy creates constraints on living personalities. On this strictly biological determination of powers, SRT is committed to self-determination and access to abortion, as well as full social provisioning for the needs of all pregnant people.

The problem is that, for Vogel, gender oppression is linked, through capitalist social relations, *only* to women's biologically reproductive powers. Vogel indeed supposed that "biological differences constitute the material precondition for the social construction of gender-differences."[13] Whereas Federici gave us a naturalism of bodies violated by capital, Vogel assumes a naturalism of biology as the key to gender. The crux of gender oppression for Vogel is then the requirement that women prepare the next generation of labor power. Vogel does not explore the relation between sex, biology, and gender in her account of oppression and, to be fair, writing in the early 1980s she would have been largely ahead of her time in doing so.[14] While accurate for many women, rooting gender oppression as a whole in biologically reproductive powers assumes too much about gender, and does so in a way that risks rendering the category "women" and women's oppression in a biologically essentialist way.[15]

The relational determination of labor powers that is so valuable in Vogel, therefore, reaches a limit in gender. Gender itself is thought in a biologically essentialist way in that biological difference is assumed to constitute the material basis for gender differentiation. Women's gender is developed neither as a site of its own constraints nor as a site for the development and exercise of powers beyond generational reproduction. Women are gendered and sexed by way of reproductive biology and, due to capitalism, are confined to a subordinate, but nonetheless necessary, role in both family and economy. Vogel never holds that women are oppressed because of biology alone, but the social elements of oppression are tied only to the way biological capacities create opportunities for women to be disadvantaged given competition in capitalist labor markets.

Now this way of determining "women" ignores the discursive, desiring, and the many different embodied, living ways of gendering that have very little to do with either one's reproductive capacities or how, on the basis of biology, one is sexed. The impoverished notion of sex and perhaps altogether absent notion of gender leaves Vogel's version of women's oppression little room to theorize trans and intersex women's oppressions. When Alyssa recalls shame "for not having [surgical] work done," and her concerns about "predatory behavior," she is describing worries that many women have had, which are only partially rooted in biology, and which are experienced in distinct ways by young trans women. To appreciate the gender oppression experienced by these women, women's oppression needs to be acknowledged in its diversity. Contemporary regimes of gendering would then need to be seen as social forces that link up with capital in constraining and violence-enabling ways.

Still, no one can be faulted for not doing everything, and Vogel's project of providing a theory that unites women's oppression with capitalism via inter-generational social reproduction is path-breaking work.

The biological capacity some have to gestate is certainly significant—it's the basis for labor power's reproduction across generations. And Vogel is not alone in recognizing the consequences. For Johanna Brenner and Maria Ramas they can be broadened:

> [A] materialist account of women's oppression simply must consider the way in which the class-structured capitalist system of production can incorporate the biological facts of reproduction, and the extent to which biological differences, considered in such a context, condition women's participation in economic/political life, their capacity for self-organization in defence of their interests and needs, and so forth. Furthermore, this problem must be approached in a historical way. We must consider how the historical development of capitalism may have altered this relationship.[16]

We can therefore follow Vogel in acknowledging that many have biological powers to gestate, and those that do, or are even presumed to have this power, are oppressed in capitalism. It is obvious that bearing children in capitalism puts one at a disadvantage on the labor market, and in other arenas. Vogel is right, women are indeed oppressed in capitalism, and a lot of oppression stems from the fact that women shoulder most of the inter-generational reproductive burden.

Yet, without ignoring biological capacities, we can also develop gender and gender oppressions beyond biology. In fact, Vogel's strategy of reading our capacities in light of enveloping social relations provides a fine model for how to do precisely that. So, even though Vogel does not address the diversity of gender oppressions, and ties women's oppression and perhaps, by implication, women too closely to biology, the model for thinking oppression she develops is very valuable.

Neither being *able* to become pregnant nor *actually* gestating is itself oppressive, even though they often entail significant bodily work. The same is true for people who develop and set in motion gendered and gendering capacities that do not conform with the gender they were assigned at birth. Both are sources of oppression in capitalist societies that require competition to actualize our powers, and which create significant advantages for cis-gendered men. Women as well as trans, fluid, and non-binary people suffer from disproportionate constraints and relations of dependence. Whether they stem from diminished physical ability to compete in labor markets or labor markets' serial reproduction of gender norms, both are sources of gender oppression.

Interestingly, these oppressions are deeply connected. Capitalist societies rely on the biological capacities for gestation in ways that are not socially supported. This means pregnancy, though part of social reproduction, is highly privatized work. This privatized approach to social reproduction, in turn, makes people who are gestating disproportionately dependent on people, generally partners, who are not. This has the effect of reinforcing the constraints of misogynistic and regressive gender norms in families organized around the wage-earning advantages of cis-gendered men.[17] Even though Vogel does not move in this direction, her concern for the gendered effects of privatized generational replacement of labor power can then be used to generate responses to both women and other genders' oppressions.

To be clear, these criticisms do not apply only to Federici and Vogel themselves. They apply to *any* theory that conceives bodies as ontologically natural, or that conceive women's oppression in a merely biological way. These criticisms of Federici's and Vogel's accounts can serve as warning signs that can help SRT develop in more compelling, even more Marxist ways.[18]

SRT can study the relational and practical forces through which engendering capacities link up with others, like our potentials to pursue sexual pleasure, develop satisfying family structures, and participate more broadly in social life. It can show that all of these are not only lived and reproduced, but that we deeply change them through their reproduction in both uneven and horizon-expanding ways. SRT can and must be committed to a relational and historical determination of sexed and gendered bodies. Yet what being a sexed and gendered body amounts to is not a whole lot until we know how our different capacities are developed and set to work.

Federici is right to show how bodies can be formed by relations of domination, and Vogel is right to insist on the specificity of women's oppression through a materialist class analysis. We therefore have some resources to read both of them against the grain. It is possible to develop a theory of social reproduction that shows sex and gender as transformed by their histories of resistance. With SRT, we can grasp the enveloping, evolving, and dominating social relations resistance throws into question, and sometimes even successfully revolts against. In this way, SRT's emphasis on our historical unfolding is well situated to show

how "natural" and biologically essentialist regimes of sex and gender are merely passing—in both senses of the term.

This social, historical, and labor power approach to our bodies as sexed and gendered points us to a theory of social reproduction that has a broad liberatory horizon. The powers of our sexed and gendered bodies are constrained and contorted by capitalist social relations, and not in equal ways. The ways we grow into our abilities to craft and express our cis, trans, non-binary, and fluid selves is almost never straightforward. Gendering in capitalism is for only the vanishingly few an easy, comfortable, or remotely fulfilling process. SRT provides the theoretical framework to understand just how and why that's the case through the ways we navigate our desires and needs in the midst of the constraining logic of capital, and the social relations that varyingly inhibit or promote our freedom. When our desires and needs are lived and reproduced in socially frustrated forms, our frustrations can prompt a political conclusion: we need different, freer social relations.

Once the commitment of SRT to a social and historical determination of our labor powers has been linked to their material consequences, form-determined constraints, and liberatory potentials, we can avoid some deep problems. We can differentiate between powers, and make critical judgments because SRT tracks the unfolding effects of our actions on our capacities in the future. SRT can avoid the deeply problematic ableism linked to so many theories that center "power" because it challenges the very form that our capacities are constrained to take when dominated by capital. Finally, SRT can move beyond naturalizing gender through reproductive powers or resistant bodies by conceiving gender as an important part of our living personalities.

Beyond the power of our bodies to resist, or our biology to reproduce, we all have some powers to determine and satisfy gender-related needs. Yet we do not all have these powers to the same degree and in the same way. Some of us are freer to develop, actualize, and reproduce powers, while others suffer constraints in compounding ways. In the following chapter I explore the most prominent theoretical approach to this compounding problem through a generous reconstruction of intersectionality. I then show how SRT provides a valuable theoretical contribution to the rich legacy of intersectional thinking.

5

Reproducing Intersections and Social Reproduction

I went to school two towns away, so I had to wake up earlier. All of this struggle just to get an education. It was really difficult for my mom to put food on the table for us. I worked in the fields, but I would also come back and cook for my siblings. I would cook for the brother that was older than me. My siblings come from domestic violence. My mom was sexually assaulted by her father and I was sexually assaulted. But after I opened up with other women, these tears have brought happiness and healing. Before, I literally could not talk about my own story. The more you talk about it, the more you find different women talking about the gender violence that they have faced. It's a domino effect. I think it's so important because it's liberating. It's a liberating form, but it's also about finding solidarity.

A lot of people think that this happens just with uneducated immigrant workers. No. It happens with people who have PhDs. I've been in different circles. Gender violence is deep and it's toxic and it's everywhere. Our main focus is uplifting the voice and leadership of immigrant woman, women of indigenous backgrounds, transgender people, and people of color, making a safe place for these individuals. Because they're often so marginalized. These conversations about gender violence and how we deal with that at workplaces, it's very new. It should not be. (Cynthia, on the pervasiveness, diverse forms, and depth of gender violence)[1]

By centering labor power, Social Reproduction Theory's social-theoretic frame is not only an alternative to other available options. It is, I will argue here, a better one. To make that argument I will look at the different theoretical framework offered by intersectionality which has reshaped the best feminist theory of recent decades. Cynthia provides an account of her life experience in a way that is ripe for intersectional analysis. The way Cynthia had to work, go to school, and cook for her siblings combined to form a specific form of disadvantage. Cynthia's class position in a class-divided society meant she had to work in the fields from an early age. Her gender in a misogynistic society meant she suffered sexual assault and was expected to do the cooking, while her physical location made gaining an education more difficult. In the same interview, Cynthia described how "she was the only one that had documents out of all my siblings," and so could immigrate while the rest of the family stayed behind in worse life-conditions. Yet, living in the US as an immigrant meant she tried "to be unnoticed."

As a way of understanding layered and multiple oppressions, intersectionality owes its force to roots in the Black feminist community. For this reason, the case for SRT would be incomplete without sincerely engaging with the insights of black feminist thinking. I will make the case that, despite intersectionality's strengths, SRT does a better job of explaining the causes of social violence. I consider SRT to be best suited to tackling the interwoven nature of oppressions in capitalist societies, as SRT highlights the essential role class plays in these oppressions. To make this argument, I want to develop a generous reconstruction of some anti-capitalist potentials that stem from the best of intersectionality.

This is important because too often, proponents of Marxist and Marxist-inspired social theories have rejected intersectionality. They have approached intersectionality as if its best forms were a regression behind truly radical theory. Intersectionality is often charged with offering only liberal methods and assumptions about identity that fail to indict and challenge capitalism. Other critics have argued that intersectionality— as used today—makes the theory appear as if its sole promise was an entirely liberal version of "identity politics."

As with SRT, there is a long and radical history that precedes the kinds of intersectionality that are commonplace today. Intersectionality has roots going at least as far back as Sojourner Truth's 1851 "Ain't I a Woman" speech.[2] A version of its social-analytic application is partially developed in W.E.B. Du Bois' 1935 *Black Reconstruction*.[3] In the twentieth century the roots of the theory were developed more explicitly through the efforts of many radical queer Black women. This history should give us pause, and help us avoid reducing the rich tradition of intersectionality to just one line of thinking. We must bear this heritage in mind while casting a critical gaze on the ways intersectionality has been taken up and distorted in contemporary consciousness.

Be that as it may, if a theory like intersectionality can be taken in so many different directions, there might be something in the theory itself that can be held at least partly responsible for these diffuse developments. Perhaps there is no singular theory, no discrete, coherent strand of thinking. To be sure, intersectionality is indeed very wide-ranging.[4] Versions of its guiding impulse have been deployed, as is clear in the Combahee River Collective's Statement, in explicitly anti-capitalist and anti-imperialist ways.[5]

But intersectionality has also taken forms that center race and gender at the cost of paying insufficient, if any attention, to how class structures capitalist societies. Without getting the classed nature of capitalist societies right, Marxists are surely right to insist that intersectionality's focus on different and compounding oppressions provides an incomplete picture. Not paying explicit attention to class risks de-centering the violently valorizing heartbeat at the center of all capitalist societies. In other words, when the exploitation at the center of the class relationship is given short shrift, the social analyses that follow can suffer from a compartmentalization in which the reproduction of different violences is at best acknowledged but never explained.

My goal here is to neither build a straw-man version of intersectionality nor select its best possible version and insist that its value stems from how much it shares with the construction of SRT on offer. I explore the promise of an advanced version of intersectionality—as well as the limits of even this highly promising version. Given the wide-ranging ways "intersectionality" have been developed theoretically and used practically, I fully acknowledge that this reconstruction is partial. When describing intersectionality here, I am offering one way to think through its commitments, and its promise.

INTERSECTIONAL SOCIAL THEORY

"Intersectional" or "intersectionality" can mean quite a few different things, depending on how the term is used. In some guises it is a theory. In others it describes a claim about some specific experiences of oppression. In still others it serves as a method for studying, representing, or practically responding to those oppressions. It is also, in its origins, no less than in its use today, a term that demands we recognize the specific plights of those who are already marginalized. Sara Salem astutely describes intersectionality as a "travelling theory."[6] If this is true, what holds this range of possibilities together under one term?

The crucial, unifying features across all of its possible meanings are the ways that being "intersectional" or using "intersectionality" in research, analysis, presentation, or struggle require:

1. Attention to the specific ways compounding harms are experienced as so many forms of violence.
2. Positing that no specific input into these compounds is primary or logically prior to any other.
3. Recognition that this diversity of suffering is felt unequally across different populations.
4. A commitment to combatting both the fact and social invisibility of this disproportionate suffering in ways that don't produce what has been called an "Oppression Olympics."[7]

For this reason, intersectionality is also a way of seeing and understanding that provides what would otherwise be a missing space for marginalized people. This seeing and understanding is then often used to sponsor a politics that centers the marginalized voices. Very broadly, intersectionality recognizes differences as a ground for solidarity and action.

None of this seems very controversial. Who could disagree with the ideas that we are all different, that some are harmed differently and in more overlapping, confounding ways, or that we ought to be aware of that fact and sensitively respond to it? Black women are harmed in a racist society for being Black, in a misogynistic society for being women, and for being Black women in a society that unites its racism and misogyny in particularly creative and nasty ways. So specifically nasty, in fact, that it has been useful to develop new terms like "misogynoir" to name this combination.[8] Not paying attention to the specific and co-constituting force of multiple oppressions impairs attempts to build solidarity. The force of multiple and combined oppressions can then be added to the intersection of gender and race. As research continues, it increasingly delineates more specific axes of social violence, and collates them in a matrix of domination.

Gender, documentation, immigration, access to education, and class all contribute to the ways Cynthia, and so many other women, experience various forms of domination in their lives. Yet they also color prospects for liberation. Cynthia is also quite clear that it was tremendously helpful to get organized, fight back, and foster a community of support. She sees this community as a venue in which her own and other women's stories could be shared and believed. Domination and the agency to fight against it that Cynthia describes are not separate from each other, but are mutually intertwining.

Patricia Hill Collins has developed the idea of a "matrix of domination" in order to capture this kind of complexity, and develop an intersectional account of social violence.[9] I take the kind of position developed in Collins' *Black Feminist Thought: Knowledge, Consciousness, and the Politics of Empowerment* to be a high water-mark for the theory of intersectionality, and use Collins' work here as a guide for my reconstruction. Her development of a "standpoint epistemology" provides a theory of knowledge rooted in Black women's understanding of their oppressions, and offers "safe spaces" as a response to oppressions. Here, however, I will focus on the idea of a "matrix." I want to develop the structure and strengths of seeing intersectional oppressions as elements of a matrix of domination.

Collins' "matrix of domination" links together different, yet intersecting forms of oppression. The idea of a matrix that unifies oppressions provides a view of the social whole while situating diverse harms. It follows that the coordinates of specific dominations can be plotted and appreciated as specifications of a larger, enveloping social order. Collins writes that

> intersectionality refers to particular forms of intersecting oppressions, for example, intersections of race and gender or of sexuality and nation. Intersectional paradigms remind us that oppression cannot be reduced to one fundamental type. This has thoroughgoing implications for how oppressions work together in producing injustice. In contrast, the matrix of domination refers to how these intersecting oppressions are *actually* organized.[10]

This describes the ambition of Collins' account, which she holds requires theoretical and lived, experiential accounts to flesh out.

Even more valuably, Collins' matrices are scalable and historical. To take scale first, oppression in a specific context is linked to the more general social organization of oppression. While Black women live through a specific matrix of domination that has more than one element,[11] "African-American women's group history becomes crafted in the context of the specificity of the U.S. matrix of domination."[12] In this way, matrices create links between different levels of domination. This is done in a way that preserves the specificity of each, and which allows them to be captured within and across other, relating matrices. The US as a social organization can be the name for a very broad matrix. Within it, US African American women's oppression can be the name for a narrower, more specific matrix.

Collins is also sensitive to the upper limit of this scalability, that is, to the way it can describe a global order. Drawing on the work of Black feminist and Marxist theorist Angela Davis, Collins holds that we need "new ways of conceptualizing oppression and activism that take class differences of a global matrix of domination into account." She further acknowledges that:

> Domination is structured differently in Senegal, the United States, and the United Kingdom. Thus, regardless of how any given matrix is actually organized either across time or from society to society, the concept of a matrix of domination encapsulates the universality of intersecting oppressions as organized through diverse local realities.[13]

Collins' matrices are scalable to the point of universality, and specifiable down to the particular violences suffered by different groups of people. Though centered on the Black women in the US, Collins' theoretical principles can flesh out matrices of domination worldwide.[14] If we accept that the US, Senegal, and the UK all relate to and influence each other—though, of course, given the histories of imperialism and colonialism not in equal ways—then fully grasping the scope of oppression requires including, but also thinking beyond the bounded nature of nation-states. For these wider, indeed globally structured and reproduced oppressions, we would need to use an internationalist framework.

At every part of their possible range, Collins' matrices also evolve and develop in new ways. For instance, a nested matrix like that appropriate to African American women is not posited as a simple fact, but as historically unfolding. What US African American women's oppression looks like today shares some consistencies with but is also significantly different from what it looked like during the period of reconstruction. Layered matrices of domination are complex, unstable structures that can help us think the varied and varying forms of domination appropriate to any level of social analysis.

Matrices of oppression inform the scope, nature, and direction of people's potentials and capacities in uneven and specifiable ways.[15] In this way, matrices of domination are not external impositions. They are constituted in part through the constrained powers of those within them. Each matrix of domination is likewise constituted within and encompassed by overlapping matrices and is linked to other matrices internally produced in similar ways. This continues all the way up the scale to a global matrix and its totality. In other words, this theory opposes mechanical notions of harm stemming from a crude notion of independent intersecting forces. In this intersectional account of a relationally determined totality, Collins' theory can be understood as comprised of stacked, scalable, and self-constituting matrices of domination.

What does it mean to say that these matrices of domination are self-constituting? Collins argues that matrices hold themselves in place, and are the causes of their own evolution. As such, matrices of domination are organizations of our power, which exists in some form no matter how oppressed anyone is. In other words, for Collins too, we all have some powers even if in contorted, diminished, or socially under-recognized ways. This is crucial because it means even the most dominated have the power to see, name, actively respond to, and link up with others in fighting their dominations. Collins writes:

> As people push against, step away from, and shift the terms of their participation in power relations, the shape of power relations changes for everyone. Like individual subjectivity, resistance strategies and power are always multiple and in constant states of change ... domination and resistance shape and are shaped by individual agency.[16]

Collins' argument that matrices of domination organize disciplinary forms of power is decisive. This perspective deepens the view that agency shapes and is shaped by historically evolving forces.[17]

Seeing, naming, and then claiming the space to construct knowledge are forms of resistance. Thinking this way affirms the power of those who have all too often been subject to domination. This epistemology, or theory of knowledge, is therefore itself a challenge to the way dominating power relations deny some the power that comes along with socially accepted forms of self-knowledge. Situated knowledge creation is an extremely important part of Collins' political commitments. Uncovering, exploring, and fostering spaces for agency against its denial inform much of Collins' relation to the history of Black feminist thought. Rather than simply describing the world as it is, this practical theory of knowledge is transversal. It is committed to "transforming unjust social institutions" in a larger politics of empowerment.[18]

This account of Collins' work shows us the strengths of an intersectional approach to oppressions. As a framework for integrating intersectional harms, Collins' "matrix of domination" is beyond the standard issue criticisms of "identity politics" leveled at intersectionality by both the right and class-reductive or class-only Marxists. Collins' "matrix" is a specifiable universal shifting through time, and comprised of further specifiable, overlapping, and evolving nested matrices. It can situate the oppressions experienced by individuals or groups with shared identities. It explains situations in view of their trajectories and illuminates how agency evolves in more or less dominated ways within a social whole. Any politics rooted in an identity would need to be linked up to others—in an increasingly universal response to the way matrices of domination are actually organized.

We should also observe that Collins' work includes a conception of "class." In fact, for Collins, Marxist notions of class are actually the starting point for the standpoint epistemology she defends.[19] Because the proletariat is the subordinate group in capitalism, it is in a privileged position to know the truth about the violent power of capital. Yet this Marxist approach is accused of being "binary," and is not nearly fine-grained enough for Collins. There are, she contends, no proletarians as such, but there are raced and gendered proletarians. The more we specify subordinate groups, the closer we can come to revealing knowing and resisting subjects.

While it is included, in this approach, class is included as just one of the many specifiable and intersecting ways of being subordinate to dominating powers. Class is, therefore, less a structure that determines power relations, and more a way that power is expressed in a dominating way. Since class itself is shot through in nested and overlapping matrices of domination, Collins shifts from a Marxist notion (tracking those who do or do not own the means of production) to a more diffuse notion of "social class." Class becomes a concept used to describe social inequality while the imperative to valorize, and the exploitation through which class distinctions are reproduced, are blurred or set further into the background.

MARXIST RECEPTIONS OF INTERSECTIONALITY

There are stark differences in how Marxists have responded to inter-sectionality. Marxist feminists in particular tend to be polarized around the question as to whether intersectionality should be regarded either as a powerful analytic resource to be welcomed or as a competing and ultimately insufficient theory. The second view sometimes goes as far as framing intersectionality as a dangerous, liberal growth that is choking the once promising life out of left analysis in both academia and cultural discourse more broadly. Martha Gimenez, for instance, holds that "from the standpoint of Marxist theory, intersectionality is a powerful ideology that obscures the meaning and significance of class and class relations, even among those who should know better."[20] For Gimenez, herself a theorist of social reproduction, "intersectionality as an academic pursuit is an approach to studying inequality in any discipline or field of studies … from any theoretical perspective *except* Marxism."[21] The two, in other words, are absolutely incompatible. Without a clear account of class, intersectionality and Marxist approaches simply cannot be mixed. Attempts to do so, Gimenez and those who share her stance suggest, are misguided at best and dangerous at worst.

Ashley Bohrer, on the other hand, is more optimistic. In *Marxism and Intersectionality* Bohrer holds that Marxists and theorists of inter-sectionality have a shared basis for critical collaboration. She suggests that through uniting forces, we could develop "a more integrated theory of intersectional capitalism."[22] Writing from an explicitly social repro-duction framework, Sue Ferguson has suggested that SRT provides the idea of the whole or social totality that would otherwise be missing in intersectionality.[23] Of course, between outright rejection and different integrative arguments, there is every possible shading of grey.[24]

This is more than yet another small squabble within a fractious academic left. If class is not clear and central, capital might be left in place as we replace anti-capitalist militancy with little more than respect for the different harms it in part causes. On the other side, when a class-centric perspective denies Black women and other already deeply marginalized people the space to articulate and fight specific oppressions, then the multiply jeopardized have yet another form of basic denial to add to the matrix. Even Marxists give them short shrift! The debates about inter-sectionality on the left are often so fraught because it can look like the mere existence of each side throws the legitimate existence of the other into question.

For their part, some intersectional theorists have not paid attention to the ways SRT is far better than reductive versions of Marxism. Collins herself has argued that Marxism is guilty of "reflecting the binary thinking of its Western origins."[25] Likewise, some Marxist accounts have indeed articulated class-only or reductive accounts of oppression.[26] At their worst, Marxist feminists have developed caricatures of intersectionality in their own self-defenses. This is why before moving to criticism or theoretical self-defense, it has been important to set out and highlight one of the most powerful version of intersectionality available.

Some critics of intersectionality from the left point out that intersectionality does not have an adequate concept of class. They tend to argue that without centering the class relations and the imperative to valorize that set capitalist societies on their paths, intersectionality re-inscribes identities in an ahistorical way,[27] and that it divides oppressions without any story about how they are caused. Moreover, the focus on oppressions sidelines the kinds of agency that could work to overcome our violent social order. While these criticisms may be appropriate against some versions of intersectionality, when leveled against Collins' position the charges simply cannot stick. Concepts of agency, historical development, compounding causes of harm, and a social whole that includes some concept of class are all present in her work.

Further, intersectionality's focus on oppression is often in the service of highlighting diverse potentialities for life-satisfying activity. Like SRT, intersectionality is concerned with how oppressed groups reproduce their existence under deeply unfavorable circumstances. Some versions of intersectionality do this through a criticism of capital as itself a limiting force on oppressed people's powers. When generously interpreted, the two theories seem rather close. What then motivates developing SRT in particular?

THE CASE FOR SRT

So far, I've shown how SRT is committed to relating the ways social forces determine labor powers to the active embodied work of so many living personalities. But where does capital's imperative to valorize fit into SRT's account of the different ways we are socially disempowered? The first step is to remember that capital's imperative to valorize is satisfied through a class relation. Capital can only valorize when capitalists exploit the powers of the working class' living, embodied personalities. Capital grows through the specific class division that requires workers to sell their powers for a wage.

The imperative that capital valorizes, and its root in the class relation, means class is not just one social relation that exists alongside so many others. Class is a relational term that, in capitalist societies, differentiates those who can satisfy their needs through what they own from those who do not own enough, and must exchange their own labor powers for a wage or depend on someone who does. The logic of this class relation describes a hard constraint on whose needs can be satisfied and how.[28] Within this logic, the satisfaction of needs proceeds so long as it advances, or at least does not seriously challenge, capital's valorization. SRT sees the class relation that enables valorization as the social institution that forms the violently beating heart of *any* capitalist society.

Regardless of how capitalist societies are then fleshed out and put in relation to each other, a society is and can continue to be capitalist only if it is organized around this class relation and the valorization it entails. The imperative to valorize colors how one capitalist society relates to others and inflects different oppressions within and between them. This means that all capitalist societies evolve and grow by maintaining and deepening the class relation at their basis. The centrality of the class-based relation and valorization permits SRT to see both the violence of the class relation and, as we saw in Chapter 2, the violence of the social relations that these valorizing processes move through. These can be internal to the working class, as is evident in the racism of so many working class white people, as well as international, as when relations of capitalist domination stem from and follow upon earlier colonial domination.[29] These social oppressions are strong because they set the rails for individual need development, capacity development, and the historical development of societies themselves.

As we saw, this imperative to valorize is made possible by the class relation which itself flows through extremely wide-ranging ways our powers and needs are differently constructed and constrained. For this reason, a social reproduction approach explores the specific ways social relations link up with class in creating so many different needs, so many different potentials for satisfying them, and then so many different ways we actually do that need-satisfying work.[30] This is why the kind of "unitary theory" SRT offers is not a flattened out or homogeneous unity. Holding that there is something consistent across all class-based exploitation of labor powers is far from claiming homogeneity across all the ways it is articulated.[31] The kind of unity SRT theorizes is simply the common capitalist basis for what is made possible and put into motion in so many differently dominating relations.[32]

Despite this, intersectionality provides valuable resources for thinking through much of what SRT is committed to. Any causal account of how social forces are experienced by individuals or groups certainly requires attention to their specific circumstances. And an intersectional social lens is set up very well to provide the needed material. Yet, one reason to value SRT is that it has the resources to take a step beyond intersectionality in developing causal explanations for social domination. Theorizing social reproduction can explain a key component of why and how socially dominating forces themselves are continuously reproduced. While intersectionality can acknowledge the historical and forceful elements within matrices of domination, it does not have a well-developed theory for what causes just this historical development.[33]

Let's go back to Cynthia's testimony set out at the beginning of this chapter. An intersectional account of her experience can start by locating her suffering in the fact that she is a working class, Chicana immigrant. Sometimes we might be satisfied with causal explanations that point to this kind of conjuncture. We rarely need to clarify the background thoughts in order to understand how this conjuncture produces needless suffering—at least not to most intended audiences. However, let's make these assumptions more explicit. Immigration is hard and its effects are often socially alienating. The US state and society Cynthia immigrated to is racist, xenophobic, heavily anti-worker, and misogynistic in myriad ways. These meanings are more or less built into the idea that "working class Chicana immigrant" describes a particular matrix of domination. So, describing a matrix of domination frequently counts as providing a causal explanation for why Cynthia and people like her are socially disempowered.

But sometimes we do want more than a conjunctural account. We might find it valuable to do more than explain specifically compounded situations. Anyone can see that class, race, gender, and nationality combine to make working class Chicana immigrants dominated and disempowered. But then we might want to pause a beat and ask: Why? Why is this conjuncture so disempowering? What has *caused* things to turn out in this way?

When we ask for these further steps, we are trying to get at more fundamental causes. Adding more specific accounts of an existing element or adding altogether new elements to the matrix does not suffice. Doing so would not provide a response to this why question—for that, something else is needed. Simply saying that there is a historical legacy also wouldn't do the trick because, while no doubt true, pointing to the fact of history does not explain why things turned out the way they did. We would need to provide a causal explanation that points to some aspect of society that can help us understand why it evolved the way it did.

Since a matrix names and relates experiences of domination, the social *causes* of those elements and their combination must be produced and reproduced. We need to know *why* they were produced, and *how* they are continuously reproduced as socially disempowering realities that have so much constraining force on people's lived, embodied personalities. This is precisely why SRT is valuable. Since a social reproduction approach explores how our powers to satisfy needs are produced and reproduced through social constraint, it provides the historical layer and causal depth missing in a merely conjunctural account.

The powers we have to satisfy our needs, and how they are then permitted or constrained from being set in motion are the starting point for SRT's deeper kind of explanation. Our societies are not set in historical motion by the unique force of great men, the unceasing flow of random accidents, or the generally accepted ideas and ideals of a given time and place. Our societies have their histories through the combined effects of all our need-satisfying activities. We make our histories first with what we have the ability to do, and then with what and how we actually produce and reproduce our lives. Since in capitalist societies, and those subject to them, the abilities we develop and then the possibilities we have for exercising them rely on capital's undying demand to valorize, the class relation is essential, and it is indeed a central part of the historical explanation SRT provides.

Marx himself made something much like this argument in a famous passage from his unfinished third volume of *Capital*. There he wrote:

The specific economic form, in which unpaid surplus labour is pumped out of direct producers, determines the relationship of rulers and ruled, as it grows directly out of production itself and, in turn, reacts upon it as a determining element. Upon this, however, is founded the entire formation of the economic community which grows up out of the production relations themselves, thereby simultaneously its specific political form. It is always the direct relationship of the owners of the conditions of production to the direct producers … which reveals the innermost secret, the hidden basis of the entire social structure, and with it the political form of the relation of sovereignty and dependence, in short, the corresponding specific form of the state. This does not prevent the same economic basis—the same from the standpoint of its main conditions—due to innumerable different empirical circumstances, natural environment, racial relations, external historical influences, etc., from showing infinite variations and gradations in appearance, which can be ascertained only by analysis of the empirically given circumstances.[34]

This approach does provide us with a framework for thinking that class is central in social affairs. But Marx does not here advance the reductive idea that the class relation between producers and owners explains everything else that is socially significant. While maintaining that there is an "innermost secret" and "hidden basis of the entire social structure," this secret or basis is influenced by the kinds of state and relations that grow out of it.

As we move from the innermost secret of class to what a society actually looks like, we should remember that Marx rejected a unidirectional notion of causality. For Marx, there is no one-size-fits-all approach to social analysis. To explain oppression in the twenty-first century, we need to actually look at environmental and racial relations as well as the legacy of "external" historical influences. Cedric Robinson's *Black Marxism* provides a model for doing this kind of reconstructive work. While in one sense outdated, the social effects of previous epoch's production relations still persist in significant, though mutated forms today. The result is "infinite variations and gradations" in social relations, needs, and need-satisfying capacities. The unavoidable conclusion is that these need to be studied in relation to their basis in the class relationship between producers and owners.

This conclusion is unavoidable because Marx is serious when he describes the relation between owners and producers as an innermost secret, and a hidden basis. In capitalism, this class relation is often quite hard to see as a shaping force. At every turn, the class-relation is naturalized, ignored, or explained away, rather than brought clearly into view. In order for this mystified, subterranean relation to reveal the truth about an "entire social structure," we need to do the work of investigating actually existing social structures in their historical development. Finally, since social structures exist only through their continuous reproduction, we need to see the class relation as both informing, and being fleshed out by the infinite gradations of social realities. Marx named only a few of these variations explicitly.

This way of conceiving class as a relation situates it as a key motor for what intersectionality sees as a matrix of domination. In fact, the structuring metaphor of a "matrix" has been used in just this way by Marxist theorists.[35] Seeing the class relation and the valorization that flows from it as the basis for a social organization and its historical articulation does not, at the same time, require discounting other forms of social domination. In fact, quite the opposite. This is because the logic of the class relation needs to be fleshed out. The forms of social oppression translate it, as we have seen, from being a merely logical relation to being one useful for "analyzing empirically given circumstances." The class relation, in other words, needs to be determined.

This works in the other direction as well. Focusing on socially given forms of domination does not necessarily mean discounting the moving force of the class relation. Cynthia expresses this when she first acknowledges that violence against women is a tremendously widespread social phenomenon, one existing across the class division: "A lot of people think that this happens just with uneducated immigrant workers. No. It happens with people who have PhDs. I've been in different circles. Gender violence is deep and it's toxic and it's everywhere." Yet Cynthia then insists that we make it a priority to talk "about gender violence and how we deal with that at workplaces, it's [the conversation] very new. It should not be." While gender violence is indeed everywhere, we need to pay particularly close attention to its manifestations *in workplaces*. That is, in places where workers are dependent on their bosses for a wage and therefore often subject to their whims.

The class relation and the ways gender violence works are inextricably connected. And both intersectionality and SRT can see that this is the case. Intersectionality tends to focus on the lived experience and differentiating force of this and more specified conjunctions. SRT, however, moves from the conjunctural facts of connection to an account of what drives the conjunction in its continuous reproduction. In this way, the class relation at the core of capitalist social organization is given priority. Yet this logical priority points to an effective cause that must be translated from its pure logic into social analysis. This requires situating class in light of the ways our powers are socially constrained by race, gender, nationality, ability, and so many other social forces.

This means that the class relation is not only, or purely, classed. SRT can follow Cynthia's lead—at once acknowledging that gender violence is everywhere, and making it a priority to explore gender violence as an important part of working class experience. In the *Grundrisse* Marx himself warrants this move to subjective conditions of experience: "The conditions enabling ... the reproduction of their life, their productive life process, are only posited by the historical economic process itself; both the objective and the subjective conditions, which are merely two different forms of the same conditions."[36] Here we see that "subjective conditions" are just one side, or one way, of expressing the productive processes and relations at play.[37]

Derek Sayer makes the same point in a forceful and elegant way in *The Violence of Abstraction:*

> Production relations are, very simply, any and all social relations which are demonstrably entailed in a given mode of production ... To put it the other way around, the production relations of a given mode are all those relations between people, in whose absence they would not be producing in that particular way ... What is, or is not, a production relation in any given instance can only be determined *a posteriori*, on the facts of the case.[38]

We do not need to choose between a broad conception of oppression and losing the specificity of exploitation. Sayer reads Marx as moving beyond only narrow and bourgeois conceptions of economic activity by "redefining 'economic' relations—and thus the 'economic sphere', or 'economic structure', or 'economic base' of society—as comprising the totality of social relations, whatever these may be."[39] The exact same approach helps when we think about the economic relation referred to by the concept "class."

Once we move from merely logical to social and experiential analyses, we see how the self-sustaining activities of the working class are determined by how capital—and resistance against it—actually develops needs, and sets powers into motion. We immediately see that there are wildly different conditions and experiences of *how* powers are set into motion. In a deeply misogynistic society, gender violence informs the class experience of women. In a deeply racist society, racial violence informs the class experience of racialized people. And, of course, the particular combination of violent forces named in misogynoir informs the class experience of Black women. As David McNally and Sue Ferguson put it,

> racialized, sexualized, gendered bodies, practices, and institutions matter: racism and sexism are *not* historical aberrations that can somehow be separated from capitalism's "real" or "ideal" functioning. Rather, they are integral to and determinant of—in the sense that they really and actively *facilitate*—actual processes of capital dispossession and accumulation.[40]

Gender violence in the workplace and gendered assumptions about who should do the cooking at home informed Cynthia's class experience, and she is far from alone. These gendered patterns are inseverable parts of how capitalism operates as a social order.

But this is far from a new thought. It was articulated quite precisely by Louise Thompson Patterson, in a 1936 article in *Woman Today*. Patterson held that "Over the whole land, Negro women meet this triple exploitation—as workers, as women, and as Negroes."[41] Patterson is not making the claim that being a woman or being Black *is itself* a form of exploitation. Rather, after exploring the working conditions of Black women in the south and the north, Patterson noticed that the experience of exploitation is both specified and magnified by the particular forms it takes for Black women workers as they offer their labor powers for a wage. The disempowering class relation is also, at the same time and in a combined way, a disempowering gender and race relation.

Class relations are affirmed when we socially analyze how they get played out between the living personalities of so many different workers and their bosses. This version of SRT is therefore closer to Ashley Bohrer's strategy of finding ways to link Marxism together with intersectionality, than it is to Martha Gimenez' radical rejection of the two as polar opposites. Yet there is an important difference between Bohrer's approach and my construction of SRT. The difference hangs on how "class" is configured.

Bohrer argues that intersectional social analyses reveal, in ways class-exclusive analyses miss, how capital dominates through oppressive social relations. This is why Bohrer is an "intersectional Marxist."[42] While it is certainly right to see capital as a single, coherent social system that cannot be reduced to purely economic notions of class, a problem arises by comparison. For Bohrer, a purely economic notion of class motivates the need for intersectionality. If class were not purely economic, but were thoroughly co-constituted by the social oppressions that good intersectional analyses offer, then intersectional insights could be appreciated as internal parts of a fleshed out notion of class.

Bohrer's version of intersectional Marxism does "not hold that class, as an isolatable economic or social determination, gives us a privileged understanding of capitalism, or at least, it does not do so any more than race, gender, or sexuality."[43] Yet this rejection is made possible exactly by the "isolatable" separation of class from its history and the ways it is fleshed out by race, gender, and sexuality. Capital's origins in slavery, colonialism, gender violence, and coercive heterosexuality are not reasons to reject the centrality of class. Through a social reproduction lens they can be understood as ways that the class relation appropriate to capitalism both started and to this day informs the ways class is experienced. At times it seems as if the marriage of intersectionality and Marxism depended, for Bohrer, on turning away from the ways SRT ties the fact of class relations to their social realizations.[44] SRT instead proposes bringing these much more clearly into view.

This does not mean that SRT is simply an intersectional Marxism. When we try to understand capitalism, we really do need to hold onto the centrality of class. And this holds in at least three senses. First, the abstract construction of the class relation is still valuable, even necessary. Stripped of all social and historical determinations, the class relation in which some need to sell their labor powers, while others buy those powers remains the "innermost secret" of any capitalist society. Capital valorizes through this class relation, which means the abstract notion of class is definitionally essential, even though a definition alone is far from sufficient. It is insufficient because a merely abstract definition of capital turns a social reality into a merely conceptual one.

The second reason class is essential is because class is not only valuable logically, but valuable for guiding social research as well. Class can never be dispensed with or set aside if we are trying to understand our social realities. In these social realities race, gender, and so much more will always be tangled up with the social relation described in the definition of class. We move from class as capital's innermost secret to investigating how the dynamics of social domination shape class into its "infinite variations and gradations." Class, in this view, allows us to see that different individual's living personalities are deeply frustrated by how our needs and capacities are developed, selected for realization, set into motion, and reproduced.[45] Without centering class relations, social theory could recognize many systems, social structures, physical infrastructures, and forms of social oppression, but we would not be seeing that these oppressions are situated as parts of the constitution and social reproduction of capitalist societies.

The third reason class is central lies in how it gets fleshed out when we move from its logical and social determination to its historical registers. This is where a social reproduction approach moves from a merely logical version or social description of "class" to a version that is rich with social histories. SRT does not only operate in generalities, but closely studies how our histories respond to and change social realities.[46] Taken together, logically and socio-historically, SRT maintains the centrality of class without being narrowly economistic. Oppressions conjoined with exploitation, and not just "identities," inform what SRT can mean by "class."[47]

Class is therefore not a common but ambiguous way of referring to one's social standing. For SRT it refers to the relation between owner and worker required to connect the means of production with labor power that would otherwise lack access to them. Yet, in their social force and in our lived experience, class relations are never only about the bald fact of powers and productive means. For this reason, "class" is best constructed when we see that the social relation it names is constituted through other relations, including relations of resistance and struggle.[48] These are determined by the deeply systemic ways race, gender, status, ability, and more inflect what we can think of as class experience. Without denying the hard logical core of class, we now have a more accurate account of how class works and lived class experiences. We can now appreciate the social forces of oppression that determine class experiences in different ways for different people.

When SRT situates this notion of class in a historical and evolving way it can produce some significant political consequences. Once other relations are integrated into how we understand the class relation we can begin to discern the tensions within the working class. As Cynthia's testimony showed us, they can be seen in racism, xenophobia, and misogyny. We can add violent gender norms and ableist prejudices to a list that is far from complete. This means that SRT can recognize divisions within the working class as parts of class experience that working class people play some role in reproducing. When we configure these divisions not merely as foreign logics tragically imposed on the working class, we immediately see the need for a working class politics to take these forms of oppression very seriously.

As Cynthia argued, struggling against misogyny in the workplace is a crucial part of working class politics. Women fighting workplace harassment as women are also, at the same time, struggling *as workers*. And since misogyny in the workplace doesn't disempower all women in the same way and with the same force, Cynthia very acutely priori-tizes "uplifting the voice and leadership of immigrant woman, women of indigenous backgrounds, transgender people, and people of color." With differently concretized parts of the working class mutually supporting each other's powers over and against domination at work, class-based solidarity—just like class itself—can be fleshed out across its internal relations rather than reduced to a single common denominator.

This reduction to a single common denominator is exactly the kind of denial Marx took his former mentor Bruno Bauer to task for in "On the Jewish Question." There, ironically adopting Bauer's voice, Marx rejects positions that suggest "you should feel the particular kind of your oppression and shame which you suffer, not as an exception to the rule, but on the contrary as a confirmation of the rule."[49] Marx suggested that it was insufficient to simply stop after asking questions like "who is to emancipate" and "who is to be emancipated?" For emancipatory thought to have substance it remains necessary to ask "what kind of emancipa-tion is involved?" and "what conditions follow from the very nature of the emancipated that is demanded?"[50]

To meaningfully pursue an emancipated society we need approaches that take into account how grand forces play out in our own lives, and those around us. A concretized approach to thinking class makes solidar-ity an internal principle of a working class politics while acknowledging that the working class is socially divided and differentiated in how it is dominated. Some more political implications of this way of thinking will be developed in the concluding chapter. In the next chapter, however, I turn to what I will be calling the socialist horizon of emancipation. This outline of emancipation can help SRT envision what the political struggle stemming from its social analysis is actually for.

6

The Socialist Horizon of Emancipation

We are *human beings*. (Anonymous West Virginian Teacher)[1]

We must continue to struggle. I invite all women migrant workers to fight. Do not be afraid ... I want all these women workers to study and eventually for there to be a way for all these women to continue to train themselves and improve their future. (Heleodora, on the pursuit of freer conditions)[2]

For Social Reproduction Theory the "working class" is historically determined through social oppressions that limit our personalities and what we can do. Ending today's class oppressions is therefore an ambitious aim and requires what I will be calling a "socialist horizon of emancipation." There are two complementary ways to pursue the socialist horizon of emancipation. One, signaled by the anonymous West Virginian teacher, is universalist. The demand that workers be treated like human beings stems from the feeling that this minimum of dignity owed to all human beings was not being afforded to them. When the teachers' unmet needs were denied even a hearing, they demanded that their shared humanity be reckoned with. The other, signaled by Heleodora, is more specific. Heleodora called women migrant workers, on the basis of their particular experiences, to struggle to improve their conditions. Heleodora works with New York City's Street Vendors Project in efforts to ensure street vendors' working conditions are safe from police violence and harassment.

The socialist horizon of emancipation requires both approaches. Like the West Virginian, socialist emancipation demands the dignity of human beings as needy and capable. More concretely, and like Heleodora, socialist emancipation requires attention to and motivated resistance against the specific conditions of parts of the working class. Socialist emancipation has to be something more than merely overcoming the division between the working and owning classes. The working class is not only classed in this sense, but classed through myriad social oppressions and lived experiences. So, the emancipation of the working class must also be emancipation from the ways specific constraints on labor powers are formed and experienced.

A thought experiment can help show how this is the case. Imagine a teacher in an underfunded public primary or secondary school in the US. This teacher is working class—she has agreed to sell her labor powers for a wage—and is likely a woman (even though her boss, the principal, is likely a man).[3] It is important to note that schools in areas with higher poverty employ higher rates of Black and Latinx teachers.[4] Since schools in the US draw part of their funding from local property values, wherever funding problems compound we also find a higher proportion of education workers who are racialized as Black and Latinx.

Our teacher, likely a working class woman, is not producing value because, by definition, public education does not create capitalist profits. Even though teachers have their students' futures in mind, a future that often includes value-productive work, public education itself does not produce capitalist value. Our teacher is still, however, deeply subject to capitalist pressures. For one, capitalists and their allies have been applying political pressure in her state to reduce their tax burden. Her experience of class is then informed by her low wages, declining funding for her school more generally, and the fact that social expenditures in her broader community have not kept up with prior levels of support, much less growing social need.

Often such factors operate in a combined way. Teachers with stagnant wages have been found by various studies to be routinely spending their limited wages on food or up-to-date reading materials for their classes. To make matters worse, our teacher's class sizes have grown, while teachers' aides have disappeared. Programs to support neurodiverse and impaired learners have been cut, along with the arts and music. On top of all that our teacher is expected to create a welcoming, caring, inclusive environment. If they can afford to do so, parents are increasingly taking their children out of public schools, sending them to better funded private schools. Of course, this is re-segregating as the parents who can afford expensive tuition are disproportionately white.[5]

The state has effectively farmed out adequate schooling to its underpaid staff. Where education is more accurately understood as the management of surplus populations, this combination of insufficient support then hits its target in creating under-prepared student populations, while in better funded areas students are better prepared to compete in labor markets or pursue further education.

Now, what would emancipation entail for a Black woman or Latina teacher whose experience of class takes place within these working and living conditions? It would be too quick to say that if only the relation dividing owners of the means of production from workers were undone, everything would be fixed. Without funding decisions subject to pressure by capitalists, more support would likely be provided for education, relieving these dire conditions. But what would this do for the de facto segregation of school districts? For the long and ongoing history of tasking women with doing extra, socially under-supported and under-recognized work?

While we can distinguish racial, gender, and capitalist violences at the level of analysis, actually responding to their lived consequences requires acknowledging that they are inseparably experienced and reproduced. Public schools prepare children in the US for participation in the capitalist workforce or exclusion from it, and they do so in racializing ways. This experience is never exclusively individual—it is a social experience, and one that changes over time. White supremacy—including physical infrastructures, environmental conditions, and long histories of oppression—give the substance to Black and Latina teachers' evolving experiences of class violence.

I do not mean to argue that if the class relation particular to capitalist valorization is undone that race and gender would continue to condition capitalist social relations. That would be impossible. Without the central class relation, there would be no valorization off the back of the working class, and indeed no working class distinguished from the capitalist to speak of. The separation between capitalists and workers essential to any notion of capitalism would be undone.

Instead, I am arguing that the different social oppressions particular to people racialized as anything other than white, and gendered as anything other than cis men, create different forms of disempowerment. It is clear that education is a crucial site for racialization and racially differentiating aspects of social reproduction.[6] We then have every reason to believe that racialization informs lived, embodied experiences, including the experience and shape of class domination. Social oppressions that shape living personalities help guide the contours of capitalist social relations beyond the exchange of labor power for a wage. They order where and in which environmental conditions people labor, live, and get educated. They constrain how different living personalities are socially recognized, and which lives are taken to matter at all. This is why, for SRT, socialist emancipation requires more than undoing the worker-capitalist class relation.

Socialist emancipation would entail overcoming not just the logic of class, but also the social dynamics of oppression attached to it. These dynamics of oppression are what make the inter-generational as well as day in and day out class experiences more damaging for some. Put simply, SRT tends to conceive of class as a social relation, not just a definition of the relations appropriate to a mode of production. This means that real emancipation entails overcoming not just the logical relation at the basis of capitalism—not just an economic order. It also requires overcoming the manifold social and more grounded, embodied determinations of the class relation as well. Trying to do it the other way around, and conceiving of emancipation at a remove from the lived, embodied experiences of those who are suffering moves social theory too far away from practical needs.

When imagining a post-capitalist future, only a highly reductive notion of class would insist that other oppressive social dynamics depend on a narrow notion of class and class alone. In such a view, the real, material world of class would be nothing more than an epiphonema, or an outgrowth of what the definition names. The view would consider oppressions such as racism and misogyny mere outgrowths of capital's central class relation, and see their harms only as magnifications of the singular and central class-relation. The brute fact that these different violences help capital valorize would be its narrow and exclusive focus.

Indeed, only a highly reductive view would hold that racial or gender oppression would entirely cease to exist with the elimination of the logical, disembodied class relation. If, in an idealist manner, one were to think the abstract definition of the class relation provided a sufficient view of the capitalist world, then all of the messy real-world class dynamics and experiences would be read as if they were simply results of what is thought in the definition. This approach would make it impossible to integrate meaningful social research, and the practical work of figuring out what real social emancipation looks like would be impossible.

However, racism, misogyny, and other forms of oppression are rather obviously much more than what the reductive view imagines. They are deep constraints upon our need-satisfying powers. They influence if, how, where, and when these powers can be exchanged for a wage, because they are also constraints on lived, embodied personalities outside of the labor market.[7] They are constraints on how our living personalities and need-satisfying powers are socially shaped. Further, just as pre-capitalist forms of social domination persist today in reorganized and capital-inflected ways,[8] it is likely that the oppressions of today would persist in a post-capitalist order. All merely logical, abstract, or class-reductive views of emancipation, therefore, prompt insufficient conceptualizations of full emancipation.[9] SRT's notion of socialist emancipation is therefore broader, and entirely justified in its breadth.

In this sense, it is utopian to insist that emancipation is accomplished simply by overthrowing the logical class relation. I mean "utopian" in a classical Marxist sense. In the *Communist Manifesto* Marx maligned as utopian versions of socialism that, on the one hand, saw "the class antagonisms, as well as the action of the decomposing elements in the prevailing form of society." Yet, on the other, and despite this vision of social decomposition, utopian socialists avoided the "historically created conditions of emancipation." They instead opted for theories far removed from—and thus only wishing to overcome—the social antag-onisms plaguing class-divided society.[10] Theories that recognize social forms of domination, but see them as entirely caused by the logical class relation are utopian in just this sense. We should not forget that the man-ifesto's ending suggests that our "ends can be attained only by the forcible overthrow of all existing social conditions."[11] As Marx makes clear in the following demand that workers of all countries unite, recognizing the need to overthrow *all* social conditions is not a distraction from, but the very goal of working class politics.

As we saw with Heleodora and the West Virginian teachers, the real emancipation of the working class from its exploitation must be uni-versal but it also, at the same time, must be social emancipations from specific oppressions. When I refer to the "socialist horizon of emancipa-tion," I therefore mean freedom in this more robust sense that unites the universal and the particular. Following its prior meanings, emancipation must include the right to participate in political processes,[12] and it defi-nitely includes release from bonds. Non- or second class citizens subject to increasingly violent state power can only really be free when fully included in political processes. The carceral state must be overturned, and political marginalization must be transformed root and branch. But socialist emancipation requires more than rejecting penal devastation and fighting for more complete political inclusion within a state.

Marx finely highlighted the limits of a merely political approach to emancipation in "On the Jewish Question." Even when citizenship is universally granted and rights to full political participation are universally affirmed, emancipation is still not fully realized. Oppressive social forces can still very much remain. In addition to private property, Marx focused on religious oppression and persecution, but he also singled out "birth, social rank, education, [and] occupation." Each of these social divisions, according to Marx, "act in their way … to exert the influence of their special nature."[13] To be meaningful, emancipation for those who are disenfranchised, barred from public office, and excluded from what remains of state recognition and support would have to be not merely political, but social as well. Equal rights to a public life need to be accompanied by overcoming multiple oppressive social forces.

Just as Marx would later, in *Capital*, describe our labor powers as part and parcel of our embodied, living personalities, in his much earlier "On the Jewish Question" Marx opposed "the decomposition of" people into unintegrated identities.[14] Since political emancipation is possible without general social freedom, even the fullest possible political emancipation for marginalized groups actually divides oppressed people into political beings on one side and social beings on the other.[15] It offers a version of freedom in one relatively narrow aspect of life (political life), while different oppressive dynamics are left in place to govern one's broader social existence. Political emancipation can perhaps offer freedom for one narrow and partial way of being in the world. But it leaves tremendous constraints and domination in place. Forms of emancipation that decompose lives into separable spheres like this, Marx was warning us, need to be replaced by a more robust version of emancipation—one that sees each of us as inseparably social beings. And we need to use that insight to fight against the conditions that lead us to think and behave in decomposing ways.

This is clearest in the very common sense yet precisely accurate claim made by soon-to-be-striking West Virginia educational workers. When the West Virginia workers were outraged by their state legislature's treatment of them, the raucous chant that went up inside the state-house was simply: "We are human beings." The demand to be recognized and dealt with as human beings, not political pawns, functions in at least two ways. The first is a rejection of the notion that the workers would be satisfied through politics as usual. They would, as they repeatedly demonstrated, not be willing to trade marginal gains for some against continued losses for others. There was something more at stake this time, something that touched on the value each individual knew they possessed.

The second is that the need being expressed could not—and *would not*—be ignored. To chant "we are human beings" along with so many others in a shared act of resistance is to draw attention to the fact, in a forceful way, that one is not being treated as such. To be treated as a human being is to have one's needs and social contributions recognized, valued, and responded to. To be treated as a human being, as we saw in the development of SRT's philosophical anthropology, is to be respected in the needs and powers of one's social existence. And if that is not happening, workers can collectively organize to demand such respect.

When the educators were responding to the West Virginian legislature's inhumane treatment they were not relying on a western, Euro-centric, or misogynist notion of the universal "human being." Their "human being" stemmed from a shared recognition that each one of them, in their diversity, was a human being that was not being treated as such. To say not "I am" but instead, "we are" human beings, is to respond to such slights, however implicitly, with a project of mutual recognition and support that tokens not just the possibility of socialist struggle, but a socialist future. And the future it signals is one organized around the respect and support for each person's powers to satisfy social needs.

This fight is what the socialist horizon of emancipation can offer. Invoking the socialist horizon of emancipation means developing and fighting for the freedom of our lived, embodied personalities. It is the emancipation of our labor powers from the needless experiences of their constraint. The working class is not reduced to the abstract definition of a relation, nor partitioned out into distinct non-relational identities as Marx worried about in the separation of our political from our social lives. The goal is genuine freedom for living personalities. That means the emancipation of each person's living personality and need-satisfying capacities. This requires recognizing that while an abstract definition of the "working class" is valid, it must be supplemented by acknowledging, centering, and responding, to lived social realities.

Since our powers for need-satisfying activity, and our needs themselves, are continuously produced and reproduced, socialist emancipation must be both a social and historical project. This historical dimension is one reason why socialist emancipation is best referred to as a "horizon." A horizon situates the world we experience and provides us with points of reference. A horizon can help provide an orienting point to move towards, and thereby a direction to move in.[16]

No figurative device is perfect, however. When they are approached, horizons infinitely recede. This might suggest that emancipatory politics are somehow an eternal struggle. But socialism is increasingly visible as an actual possibility. Though learning some hard lessons about lesser-evilism, parliamentary tactics, class independence, capital's international mobility, and international institutions, socialists of many stripes have moved on from the twentieth century. We are at least a generation beyond a world dominated by the implosion of the USSR, and the triumphalist view of liberal "democratic" capitalism as the unavoidable end of history.

Since the fight for socialism is back on the table, we need to ask what the fight is really for. The fight for socialism is always a fight for emancipation on two fronts. First, it is a fight *against* the social structures that constrain our lived, embodied personalities. It is resistance to limits placed on our need-satisfying powers. Second, it is a fight *for* any and all of the social structures that would condition the greatest possible direction and development of the same. It is the emancipation of our lived, embodied personalities through the creation of the structures we need to advance our freedom.

These struggles can be thought of as a fight for all that we need to be the authors of our own social reproduction. The negative fight against domination, and against the use of our powers for capital valorizing ends, is essential. But socialist emancipation requires, at the same time, a struggle for the beneficial structures and institutions that we can both lean on and develop through. Crucially, our powers to organize social reproduction must include the powers to arrange the institutions of our freedom.[17] As such, the powers and personalities that flow from such a radical transformation would be quite different from those we find today. The need to select and direct our powers would be guided by a shared recognition of our human standing, and a shared demand for our flourishing.

If we can make such a world, we would not be bound by the need to exchange powers for the cash needed to continue existing. In the broadest sense, the requirement that our institutions be rooted in the fact that "we are human beings" demands that we pursue a socialist horizon of emancipation against this capitalist form of domination. The demand is for institutions that are responsive to our needs themselves rather than their own needs for revenue or profit. It is a demand for the humanization of social reproduction.

Beyond this general definition, what socialism amounts to must be developed by the communities that fight for it. The fight for socialism by Indigenous peoples, for instance, responds to the history of dispossession. It is a struggle for land and self-determination and against genocidal state power. The fight for socialism by those dominated by capitalist state imperialisms includes struggles for political independence and self-determination, often for and through wielding independent state power. The struggle for socialism by Black women in capitalist states has and continues to be a struggle against the ways capitalist class relations vis-à-vis the state reproduce structural anti-Black racism, misogyny, and misogynoir.[18] In each and every instance, forging paths for social self-determination is the goal. But what that looks like varies according to the different forms and histories of domination being fought.

While what the socialist horizon of emancipation will look like depends on where one stands, no individual or community exists in isolation. The work we do to satisfy our needs mobilizes our communities. It requires us to participate in a thick web of connections. The teacher who needs social support to teach well also needs social support more broadly. From degraded physical infrastructure and over-policed neighborhoods, to combatting the legacy of redlining, poor environmental conditions, and malicious lending in housing, our teachers' struggle for socialism expands outward. To struggle for socialism at work is to struggle for improved education for all of her students, and forms a part of a broader struggle against white supremacy. Struggling against the broader conditions that shape her experience of class links her up with her community against all the forms of domination arrayed against her in her environment.

These connections can be developed even further afield. Social ties from one community to another are shot through with forms of disempowerment and constraint that I have hardly scratched the surface of. Marx's prohibition on decomposing our lived, embodied personalities into segmented pieces, only one or a set of which is promised emancipation, also reflects the impossibility of achieving genuine emancipation in any single, isolated community. Socialism in one community or one country is therefore not only insufficient—it is a contradiction in terms. While always approached from where one stands, socialism has to be in principle connective.

My view opposes more partial recognition of these dangers closer to home. Some socialists advocate a bounded and isolating version of "socialism." Instead of reproducing a violent global order or set of relations between communities, each community (whether a culture or a nation-state) should hermetically seal itself. Through border patrols or flattening out differences, they should avoid committing or suffering the violences of foreign contagion or internal fracturing. Or so the argument goes. Yet, such a view denies the potential wealth offered by richer, more connected sets of social relations.

By insisting on the integrity of living personalities, and our communities as evolving and inseparably connected to others, we can keep full socialist emancipation in sight. The socialist horizon can be understood as opposed to any and all social dynamics that offer more freedom or power to some slices of existence, at the cost of accepting unfreedom or domination in others.[19] Such a sacrifice is always an anti-socialist one. The West Virginia educators, for instance, refused to accept their funding increases via cuts to other social programs. For Heleodora's Street Vendors Project, the goal is not pushing police onto other workers, but less policing overall.[20] The price of freedom can never be the violent division into some that deserve it, and the construction of some undeserving set to be sacrificed to the former.

When education workers go on strike, they often do so not only for higher wages or better benefits. Beyond personal advantage, strikes have been waged for smaller class sizes, improved conditions for students and co-workers, and for better funding so that every school can have librarians, social workers, and nurses. The struggle to not be harassed by the police while working is also part of the fight to be treated like a human being. And the demands that migrant women workers make to improve their future can, at the same time, be part of a wider struggle within one's community, and for one's community to be treated with the same dignity as any other.

Struggles that do not make these more global connections are often less effective. This is because narrower aims often fail to expand to broader communities. Educators' strikes in Chicago and West Virginia could be highly successful where others were less so in large part because the teachers did an excellent job of showing how their working conditions were at the same time their own and the surrounding community's living conditions. The struggle for high quality education and housing fought by Chicago public school teachers was, at the same time, a struggle against anti-Black racism, women's oppression, and the racist city as a whole.[21]

So far I've stressed that socialist emancipation must be individual because it is linked to our lived, embodied personalities and because it demands that the powers we have are free and self-directing. In one sense, this emphasis on the individual is justified. Yet, the only way to truly free individuals is through a coordinated, socialist transformation of social relations. Existing social relations of production—in far more than the logical sense—form, set in motion, and constrain individuals' powers. Yet, this raises a puzzle. How can self-directing freedom be reconciled with the fact that our capacities are thoroughly social, and not individually made? If the only way to free powers from their reproduction in violent forms is to subject them to social control, then what kind of freedom is that? What kind of individual freedom is even conceivable once we acknowledge the fundamentally social source and nature of labor powers?

SRT needs to be able to combine both individual freedom and the social construction of our powers. And this has to be done in a compelling way if it is to avoid serious problems. Leaving the individual and the social as distinct and separated can present us with negative consequences. On the one hand, focusing on individuals without centering how powers set in motion create and reinforce social paths of domination risks liberal, even libertarian productivisms or vague moralisms.

In *The Socialist Manifesto*, for instance, Bhaskar Sunkara offers a clearly liberal and moralistic definition of what makes one a socialist. For Sunkara, one is a socialist if one recognizes each individual's moral worth.[22] But definitions relying on inherent moral worth are often used to bolster capitalist ideologies which Sunkara's manifesto is meant to serve as a weapon against. Socialists do not need to deny individual "moral worth," but recognizing it is hardly a sufficient definition of socialist commitments. This moral approach makes the socialist horizon into a realization rather than a transformation of the powers afforded to us in already existing conditions. For Sunkara, "if all human beings have the same inherent worth, then they must be free to fulfill their potential, to flourish in all their individuality."[23] Yet, in Sunkara's view, potentials are not themselves subject to radical transformation. We are offered unrestrained individuality, as if the scope and powers of the individuality capital leaves us with set the upper limit of what we can hope for.

From this moral perspective, what the wage relation does to individuality itself is nearly impossible to thematize. This is perhaps why, despite the "we need socialists" section in the concluding "How We Win" chapter of Sunkara's *Manifesto*, we find neither a clear account of what being a socialist is nor what a socialist order really amounts to. The focus on individuality ends up construing socialism's horizon as an indefinite extension of the liberal same. Focusing too much on the individual ignores how we are socially formed, and how our powers and ourselves can be socially transformed.

On the other side of the coin, however, over-stressing the social sphere at the cost of the individual is no less dangerous. Many of the twentieth century's "actually existing socialisms" were not classically capitalist, but neither were they fully socialist. Their planned organization of production did not free individuals to develop their living personalities and powers, nor were most able to participate in planning their use. It is true that labor powers were no longer subservient to a capitalist labor market, and so took on a different form. They were not commodified in the way they are under conditions of capitalism. Rather than being fully freed, however, living personalities were sacrificed for the survival of a social organization and state that, far more often than not, was socialist in name alone.

Indeed, many attempts at socialism failed to be truly freeing. Things could turn out this way because constraining the freedom of capital is not necessarily the same as freeing individuals' living personalities. The two are not opposed poles, or in a zero-sum relation. Capitalists often enough demand the anarchy of the market economy rather than production based on a social plan. They do so with the well-worn trick of conflating individual freedom with the freedom of capitalist competition. Yet, socialists need not take this bait in reverse and conflate individual freedom with the freedom to conform to a strict social plan or self-professed workers' state.

One of the essential problems with capital, after all, is that its manner of construing value renders so many specific labor powers as if they were abstract. It does this by measuring our unique capacities and living personalities via a single standard: a price for directing them, which is to say, a wage. Socialists reject this pricing of our labor powers. Wage relations reduce us all to a single common denominator and structure a society in which we measure value according to a quantifiable standard. Socialists insist that our value is not best measured by a wage, and our freedom not best constructed as what a wage would allow us to do.

But what is the alternative? Socialist emancipation rests on a form of social organization that respects each individual as a unique living personality with a unique set of powers. It would hold that we are harmed by capital's abstract valuation of our living personalities via a wage. The wage homogenizes unique living personalities by measuring our value in a quantifiable and reductive way. Through the wage, capitalist societies value our labor powers as commodities, and like all commodities our labor power is split. On one side, our living personalities and powers can be regarded as valuable in their own right. On the other, this value is reduced to a wage required for its reproduction. A socialist society, however, would not see us as commodities, but as organic wholes. Our social, living personalities would be the basis for an entirely different arrangement of what is valuable. Independent of market exchange and reductive measures of value, the diversity of our living personalities would be directly valuable, and our work would produce valuable things themselves.

Much of the work of "seeing" the socialist horizon finds its origins in Marx. When he imagines "a community of free individuals," he imagines "production in common, in which the labour power of all the different individuals is consciously applied as the combined labour power of the community." He continues to say that, "everything produced," in such a system would be "simply an object of use."[24] A useful thing would command no price or wage because we would value the thing itself, and not what it could be exchanged for. In a socialist society we would be producing and reproducing for need-satisfaction, not for exchange-values measured by a price. And since labor powers are our living personality's need-satisfying capabilities, they would be the absolute center of a socialist order. When set in motion, socialist labor powers would continuously reproduce the basis of socialist values. The very idea of labor would be transformed, and our unique living personalities empowered by such labor would be experienced in freer ways that are likely beyond what we can even imagine today.

By recognizing that we are unique and that this uniqueness is socially produced, socialist freedom must be the freedom to participate in producing and reproducing both ourselves and our societies. Freedom is not realized in the individual set against a dominating society. Socialist freedom would be a continuous, self-reproducing process of empowering individuals to contribute to social formation in ways that best realize their own need-satisfying powers. Put differently, socialism must be a flexible set of social institutions that both responds to the restraints of oppressive social dynamics and creates the infrastructure through which we could move beyond them.

This infrastructure would have to be sustainable and actualize our powers in ways that do not continue to wreak havoc on the natural environment. While not a social relation, the environment is itself conditioned by how we produce and reproduce our capacities and needs. Capital continues to be extraordinarily destructive of other life forms, delicate webs of life, and the conditions for our own flourishing. The effects of this devastation only exacerbate already existing oppressions. For this reason, socialist emancipation cannot be more of the same unrestrained development and actualization of our powers. Wherever doing so would further destroy environmental conditions or block attempts to redress growing environmental disadvantages, our capacities would require careful and coordinated restraint.

The socialist horizon of emancipation is the possibility of a connective, empowering arrangement of life. It would be the realization of potentials that, under existing circumstances, cannot yet be oriented towards their actualization. This possibility is real, but it is not already fully present. Our self-fulfillment is not simply waiting to be unearthed and grow into its mature, final form. This way of being present at a remove does not mean that socialism is a free-floating, utopian idea. It means that, no matter how rich or poor our exploited grounds are, we have to make socialism with what we have.

This work is necessarily social. And it must change over time as revolutionary potentials develop. Class reductionist views that single out class in its logical purity as the sole source for socialist struggle, and liberal, morality-based accounts both miss the essentially social nature of our powers and the lived, experienced, and thus changeable ways we can make them. They therefore risk misconstruing socialism as only an enabling mode of production rather than a set of truly liberated and empowering social relations. For SRT this more robust socialist horizon of emancipation must be pursued with a more holistic methodology—one that sees revolutionary potentials developed and navigated by historically and socially situated agents.

7

Social Reproduction Theory
and Political Strategy

[The union will continue to fight] because racism is a national trend … Students are told to grin and bear it because we do not find value in their communities … Teachers—because it is a profession dominated by women—are told to grin and bear it, because never in the history of our society have we respected the work women do. So I think yes, we will continue to see teacher rebellions across this country because sexism is still what it is, racism is still what it is. It's my hope teachers everywhere continue to see their voice as an asset, and their ability to withhold their labor as their power. (Chicago Teacher's Union Vice President, Stacy Davis-Gates)[1]

I'm an Arizona native and please forgive me for being asleep my entire life … Red for Ed has awoken my spirit of justice, truth, love, and respect for all people. I will not return to my previous slumber but fight for the many with little against the few with much. (Anonymous Arizonan teacher)[2]

While a commitment to the socialist horizon of emancipation is already a certain kind of political implication, the agents and tools through which we can pursue it remain to be developed. Simply defending a social theory, or showing that a set of political implications flow from it, is a far cry from working to bring about the theory's promise. That work requires political strategy, which is developed through hard choices about priorities, and the agents who make them. So far I've argued that Social Reproduction Theory is both analytic and critical—it can describe society, as well as pass judgment on it. I've also shown that it is a forward-looking theory because the critical judgments it makes commit it to a robust, socialist notion of freedom. But socialism is not achieved through analysis and criticism alone.

Fortunately, SRT does have strategic resources to realize its socialist goals, and they are rooted in some of the lessons learned from working class struggles like teachers' strikes. Practical struggles rather than detached efforts to refine a theory are the schools through which strategic powers for socialism are acquired. So, if SRT is to be truly practical, it needs to home in on how socialist potentials have actually grown and can continue to develop. Along with the Chicago Teacher's Union Vice President, Stacy Davis-Gates, we can see the potency of teachers' strikes, and along with an anonymous Arizonan teacher we can see how strikes motivate a political will to fight alongside one's fellow workers for a better world.

SRT travels in this practical and strategic direction because it has emerged and gained force in relation to these teachers' and other social struggles. In the course of struggle, movements often develop a need for self-understanding and refined strategic orientations. They develop insights and techniques that can help reflect on how, why, and where their movement is developing. Eleanor Marx was right to see that the liberatory force of the "woman question" could be developed only to the extent that working class women were at the head of the nascent feminist movement. The more working class women took part in feminist struggles, the more responsive their theoretical approaches would be to the dominating logic and social relations of capitalism. When feminist struggle is dominated by bourgeois women, theories tend to be developed in counter-productive ways and we end up with at best liberal feminisms.

When, on the other hand, the feminist movement develops a powerful working class orientation, as is the case in Argentina, Chile, Mexico, Spain, Poland, and Iceland among other places, space is created for a more radical way of posing and answering theoretical questions. Indeed, the more the oppressed and exploited want to be clear-sighted about their conditions and its causes, the more force radical theory will have. Yet no matter how "revolutionary" a theory is, more is required. If it does not satisfy the intellectual needs of a movement, then it will be revolutionary in a hollow and merely theoretical sense. Theory, as Marx wrote, really must "grip the masses." In order to do this, it must get to the very root of our humanity and our problems.[3]

The quotes that started each chapter centered working class women's struggles. In doing so, they have helped illustrate and concretize some of the lived, human experiences that SRT can help theorize. By drawing from striking education workers as well as from women striking on

International Working Women's Day, these testimonies came from people actively striving to develop working class power. By reflecting on their struggles, these women have already begun the theoretical work of self-clarification. These voices have helped us concretize SRT because each voice reflected working class struggle from her own vantage point. The concerns that each voice brings to the fore could not be satisfied by liberal feminisms focused on inclusion within the simultaneously exploitative and oppressive nature of capitalist social relations. Only a militant, working class, and struggle-oriented version of feminism can speak to their concerns.

This is the case even when the particular campaign each speaker was involved in might not have looked like working class struggle as it has been traditionally understood. In their political developments each sought to broaden the kinds of workplace actions that can help develop powers for socialism. Since so much of the working class works outside of the formal economy, or does not have reliable access to it at all, a working class struggle for socialism that only focuses on traditional industrial actions in value-producing sectors would be severely limited. By understanding the working class as engaging in unproductive, and even entirely uncompensated work in the home, SRT offers a notion of the working class that transcends these narrow limits. We cannot accept any approach that cuts itself off from tremendous potential resources for growing political power found in the struggles referred to throughout this book.

Yet proponents of SRT have had significantly different strategies for how to best broaden working class struggle. And for good reason. The practical implications of SRT cannot be a one-size-fits-all approach precisely because it is finely aware that what the struggle for socialism looks like will depend on the needs and powers of those doing the fighting. Pluralism has its limits, however. The crucial and common thread lies in how SRT centers historically developed needs and our self-empowering strategies for satisfying them. These are what set our living personalities and need-satisfying powers down their paths. By tapping into SRT's awareness that our needs and powers are socially produced and reproduced over time, social reproduction theorists can offer some strategic suggestions for social intervention. In other words, the key to SRT's social analysis and social criticism is also the key to its practical, strategic efforts to pursue the socialist horizon of emancipation. Even though our powers can be directed by a society that demands capital valorization, they can also be used to pursue socialism.

To avoid any potential misunderstanding, it is important to clarify what I mean by a "power." Our abilities to resist capitalism and struggle to build the freedom promised by socialism are powers. But they are not exactly "labor powers." This is because the result of their exercise is not really a use-value of some description. After all, resistance is often a struggle against the forces that reduce our living personalities to commodified labor powers. And since "use-value" is a distinction that helps us understand capitalist social orders that divide use-values from exchange-values in commodities, the entirely different social order of socialism could not be a "use-value" in any meaningful sense. The struggle for the socialist horizon of emancipation will exceed our current conditions, the nature of capitalist commodity production and as a radically different social order it cannot be fully accounted for using terms appropriate to the production of use-values.

Despite the specific meaning of "labor power" as creating "use-values," resisting a bad social order and fighting for a better one must, in some sense, rest on our capacities. These are the forces our struggles draw on, which make social change possible, and enable us to picture a better world beyond it. If socialism is a possibility, and one that is neither entirely up to chance nor brute necessity, then it has to be up to us to produce it. This is why SRT's critical understanding of capitalist societies is also a hopeful vision. SRT sees that the construction of labor powers under conditions of capital is exploitative and oppressive in myriad ways, but in the same breath it sees that this logic and social order can be challenged. We can distinguish between the meaning of "labor powers," as a concept useful for understanding the production of use-values, and the powers we have to make social orders. We can call the second form "political" powers.

By using political powers as powers to refashion our social order, we can move beyond narrow political approaches to freedom. We do not need to limit ourselves to the conventional notion of political activity. Voting, campaigning for elected officials, and even personally running for office are "political" in the narrow sense. When these exercises of our powers work by accepting the existing political infrastructure and capitalist order, then they are narrowly political. This remains the case even when these powers are used for ostensibly "progressive," self-professed "radical," or even "socialist" causes. When successful, we get at best a softer administration of the capitalist social order with perhaps some semblance of acceptance, inclusivity, and social welfare funded by taxing the profits of capital. What we do not get is a fundamental challenge to systematic social oppressions and exploitation. Without challenging the social order in a robust way, this narrowly political strategy ensures that we continue reproducing oppressive and exploitative relations.

The actions appropriate to our conventional political lives are not necessarily so narrow. Under certain conditions, and when pursued in a certain kind of way, they can be exercises of our political powers to radically reshape our social order. This is the case when things like voting, campaigning, and running for office actually pursue a socialist horizon of emancipation. This is also the case when these actions are done in a way that grows our capacities to realize socialist emancipation. Since SRT is committed to a radically different social order, it can welcome some kinds of electoral work. But SRT's strategic orientation is not exhausted by such work. The most important question to ask is whether political work or, for that matter, any exercise of our powers, grows our capacities for socialism, or not.

How can we know what kinds of struggles grow our powers for socialism? In the abstract, things are not at all very clear. In the US, will socialists working in a left-leaning democrat's campaign for public office find valuable points of contact and foster relationships with people who may be increasingly open to actually fighting for socialism? Or will those working for a democratic candidate end up making people accept and relate to the democratic party as the upper limit of what is possible? Socialists do not speak with a single voice on this issue.

Since SRT aims to transcend capitalism, its analysis of social conditions requires figuring out what would best grow our powers for pursuing and realizing socialism. SRT has two further questions that can guide socialists as we approach these and similar questions of strategy. Though I will develop them sequentially, in actual political work the two questions are interwoven and inform practice at the same time. The first question is the question of *who*. Theorists using a social reproduction view ask ourselves *who* is charged with socially reproducing our needs and powers. This *who* of social reproduction keys into who makes and continuously remakes—both individually and inter-generationally—the embodied, living personalities by which we have and can satisfy our needs. Strategically, the *who* question is often used to help identify the workers essential to a capitalist social order, but who are also not directly exploited by capital, organized, or even properly recognized as workers in the first place.

SRT responds to this kind of *who* question by tracing out how the powers that enable capital to valorize are generated in highly gendered, and highly gendering ways. The labor power that gets exploited by capital is not itself naturally given. It is always embodied in living human beings. Any workforce is made up of workers who need nurturing and care. It is no surprise then that this kind of work is disproportionately borne by women. Yet we might pause and wonder why this gendered division of labor is not more surprising. Why is it the case that women tend to do this socially reproductive work?

In many strains of SRT "socially reproductive" work is thought of as just a loosely related family of work that women tend to do. Indeed, women are usually tasked with taking care of and developing embodied labor powers.[4] In this way, some lines of work become gendered as "women's work." To many, it feels natural to think of some kinds of work in this gendered way. SRT sees this "natural" feeling as a key part of the social production and reproduction of gendered expectations. And these expectations, in turn, help shape existing realities. While never strictly reserved for women, the work done by midwives, nannies, babysitters, early childhood educators, housekeepers, waiters, sex workers, nurses, social workers, home health-care aides, and dental hygienists, to name just a few lines of work, are generally thought of as women's work. While they have historically not always performed by women, for the time being, these are lines of work in which women are indeed the majority.

SRT's response to the *who* question strategically centers women's work. Whether exploited and producing surplus-value or not, "women's" forms of work are crucial to reproducing the labor powers at the heart of our capitalist social order. The insight that comes from answering "disproportionately women" to the question "who most directly reproduces our labor powers?" centers women's work and working class women's struggles as strategically important. This is appropriate in light of the willful social blindness to heavily gendered and often unpaid forms of labor.

The capitalist organization of socially reproductive work would itself need to be overthrown and socialized, if women currently doing socially reproductive work are to enjoy the full socialist emancipation. If we are to be free to pursue work that best realizes the needs of our living personalities, even more is required. The general social assumption that there is a naturally gendered division of work itself must be overcome. Women workers are therefore a key part of the struggle for socialism. This is because without socializing women's work we wouldn't have socialism at all. As is the case with other lines of work, the struggle to make social reproduction of labor powers socialist should be fought at the points of (re)production, by those who do it.

This is not merely a theoretical point. SRT centers women as strategic agents because women can take steps to challenge their constraints, including the socially constructed gendered constraints on women's work. As an under-organized but potential force for socialist emancipation, women doing socially reproductive work are already politically active. It is no accident that feminist mobilizations are on the rise, nor that the growth in radical protests around the world have often been led by women. SRT is therefore committed to feminism in a distinctly socialist form, as a constitutive part of the socialist horizon of emancipation.

SRT's socialist feminism does not simply seek to advance women in the workplace. Nor is the agenda limited to gaining more recognition and compensation for women's work outside formally recognized workplaces. In the final analysis, these would amount to the liberal versions of feminism. When I hold that SRT's feminism is a socialist feminism, I mean that it throws into question the very social order through which the reproduction of our powers is arranged. It does this by strategically centering the most powerful weapon of the working class, that is, the strike. Politically SRT can be, and often is, committed to developing social reproduction strikes. These are strikes in which the specificity of women's labor powers are brought to the fore. Camille Barbagallo put the point forcefully in her discussion of the International Women's Day strikes:

> The very fact that reproductive labor is what keeps us and those we love or are paid to care for alive means that reproductive labor cannot be refused. Under the current conditions of capitalism, reproductive labor can only be redistributed either through processes of commodification or to someone else in an unwaged capacity.
>
> In bringing together a politics that confronts women's work in both its productive and reproductive capacity we are able to confront the impossibility of the women's strike with something else: a demand for the reorganization not only of production but of reproduction ... We have to collectively refuse to continue to offer our labor, our services and our care to those who seek only to maintain their power and profits. We strike to make our power visible.[5]

International Women's Day strikes help politicize women as both workers and as women at the same time. They offer a way to manifest, recognize, and grow commitments to working class struggle. They achieve this through re-popularizing the strike as a viable tool for working class women's political thinking and practice.[6] In doing so, they help provide a socialist stance on gender where previously liberal discourses and practices were dominant. They provide radical expressions of discontent, and offer a shared, connective means for combatting working class women's constraints in the midst of oppressive capitalist societies.

SRT's strategic insights can take this breakthrough a few steps further. The kind of work thought of as "women's work" can also be used to highlight and challenge how the work women do reflects on the ways *gender itself* is socially produced and reproduced. There is a kind of ongoing feedback loop between the dispositions, skills, activities, and arrangements appropriate to the kinds of work that women tend to do and our assumptions of masculine or feminine ways of working. What we regard as men and women's natural ways of being in the world are intimately tied up with the demands of respective workplaces. The way women's fields of work tend to be gendered then reproduce not just labor powers and our society more generally, but gender distinctions appropriate to "women" themselves.

These distinctions are anything but stable. As the skills developed and kinds of work women tend to do changes, some of our gender distinctions become unsettled. This might occur through sudden changes in labor pools as was the case during World War II, or more gradually over time, as was the case with computer programming, which was once much less dominated by men. The way we tend to divide work along gendered lines, in other words, also plays a role in the loose and historically changing configurations of gender itself.

Recognizing the malleability of gender in women's work has tremendous implications for SRT's relationship to queer struggles for socialism. Trans men, trans women, intersex, and non-binary people suffer disproportionately high unemployment rates because workplaces are often inhospitable to (or simply do not hire) people who are not cis gendered. Precisely because SRT can see women's oppression as tied to the *evolving* patterns of gendered work, it can also give the lie to assumptions that gender is a strict and closed binary. And once gender as a natural binary is thrown into question, SRT opens space to center not just cis women's struggles, but many forms of gendered resistance.

The line determining what counts as "women's" dispositions, capacities, and activities is produced in a fuzzy way. Since gender changes over time through resistance and evolving patterns of work, then in a meaningful way, womanhood itself is better read as a mutable social constellation rather than a brute fact. Tying the social construction of gender itself to the ways we work can motivate working class women's responses to women's oppression. The same then also holds for working class trans, intersex, and non-binary responses to the constraints on, or impossibility of, queer working class lives as well.

Developed in this way, SRT's response to the *who* question, reveals other forms of gender oppression, that is, the gender oppression arrayed against so many queer people. These oppressions can be overt in the outright refusal to hire or make workplaces accessible (and non-violent) for gender non-conforming people. It can also be more insidious and hidden. Trans, intersex, and non-binary gender oppressions are sometimes blatant (as with street harassment or police violence), but more often are rendered invisible through unemployment, homelessness, and social isolation.

Since trans men and women, intersex, and non-binary people have compounding and different challenges at work, different forms of gender oppression must be considered parts of working class experience. Many people in these positions are not able to sell their labor powers for a wage on any regular basis. For this reason, the way SRT considers the who question, when consistently followed through, directly ties its socialist feminist response to women's oppression to a queer socialist response to trans, intersex, and non-binary oppressions as well. SRT's socialist feminism recognizes that our fight for socialism must center and respond to the emancipatory needs of trans, intersex, and non-binary members of the working class. SRT's socialist feminist is therefore and necessarily a queer socialist feminism.

This is why so many social reproduction theorists roundly reject forms of feminism that exclude trans people. And since a disproportionate number of trans women—especially Black and Latina trans women—are pushed towards sex work (due to being excluded from formal waged labor) the same logic commits practitioners of SRT to supporting sex workers' struggles.[7] The recent International Women's Strike in the US, for instance, was organized in part by social reproduction theorists, and expressly demanded labor rights for domestic workers, but also crucially for sex workers.[8]

Given its understanding of labor powers SRT is committed to acknowledging sex work as a kind of work. It also appreciates the compounding racial and gender oppressions that push some more than others towards this line of work. Doing so responds to the who question by clarifying lines of composition within the working class. This shows us who, though far too often excluded, must be a part of the class struggle for socialism. Socialism has to include freedom from racialized and gendered coercions into more dangerous forms of work. And that includes, but is not limited to, sex work. This, in turn, means creating space in socialist movements for those actually doing such work.

In this way, SRT's *who* question denaturalizes the role women play in the reproduction of labor powers. This is a step towards also denaturalizing different forms of gender oppression and gender itself. Crucially, SRT links women's struggle against a hierarchical form of gender oppression to struggles against forms of gender oppression that stem from binarism. While women can be trans, intersex, non-binary, or all three at the same time, the overarching point is that gender is in part informed by one's activities. Gender therefore forms an inseparable part of one's working class experience and living personality. As a Marxist theory, SRT can promote emancipation from the violence of gender as part of one's class experiences, and includes in its strategic view the need to organize around different forms of gendered class disempowerment.

Yet denaturalizing gender through changing patterns of working and organizing is not enough. After all, some feminists acknowledge that gender is socially constructed rather than natural. But they then twist this point to deny that trans men, and especially trans women are legitimately their stated genders. They usually forget about intersex people, or relegate them to oddities. When someone socialized as a boy or man comes out as a woman, the trans-exclusionary position holds that this is at best a regrettable confusion—or more likely a lie. For SRT this is unacceptable because being a woman is comprised of an evolving but loosely bounded set of need-satisfying activities, modes of appearance, and self and other-regarding desires. We are strongly pushed into these overarching patterns from childhood, but it does not follow from this that people who are socialized as boys rather than girls cannot grow up to be women.

SRT is opposed to any feminism that would deny powers for gender affirmation. We can respond to its violent denial of the freedom to gender oneself by turning to SRT's second strategic question. The second strategic question moves from asking *who* to asking *what* we produce, and continuously reproduce. SRT's response to the *what* question is that individually, socially, and inter-generationally we produce and continuously reproduce our practical, need-satisfying powers or capacities. These powers in the service of use-values are "labor powers." But they can also take the form of radical, socialism-pursuing political powers. Since this insight is directly related to SRT's strategic response to gender oppression, I will start there. But the force of this *what* question has wide-ranging consequences.

Genders as I understand them are socially produced and reproduced. But this social reproduction, like any other, is the combined result of our social activities. We, in other words, are the makers of gender. We do so through our dispositions and activities, and these activities can be nothing other than realizations of our powers.[9] This is to say that we have the powers to make and continuously remake gender. And this is the case even when the conditions in which we can develop and exercise our powers are, due to the sedimented weight of traditions that often weigh like nightmares, far from the conditions we would most prefer.[10] Even under the most regressive and violent regimes of gender control, we always have at least some self-engendering powers.

We have these powers because the individual is not a discrete unit or pole absolutely opposed to and therefore merely subject to social forces. Each of us is also a bearer and potential source of social power in our own right. Each one of us contributes to the combined effects of a social regime of gendering. And we do so through our own capacities for determining our relationship to the possibilities of gender in our social organizations.[11] Even under intense normalizing pressures, and perhaps even *especially* under such pressures, the creative force and social organization of resistant engendering powers comes to the fore.[12]

SRT's attention to powers and capacities keys into this highly circumscribed power for self-determination. Even when deeply constrained by families, possibilities for work, the state, regressive medical cultures, and compounded by oppressions due to race, disability, immigration status, and the rest, some self-determining powers persist. We have some powers to arrange our gendered living personalities and social organizations in freer ways. When confronted with gender binarism trans, intersex, and non-binary people draw on gendering powers to defy gender norms for both personal and social ends. These social ends are important because the individual alone cannot reorganize gendering relations in capitalist societies. Beyond affirming chosen genders, many intentionally foster social relations through which the need-satisfying powers of queer people can flourish. Such work has been referred to as "queer social reproduction." This is not just the processes queers use to stay alive; it seeks to safely expand the scope of gender freedom.[13]

In this queer sense, social reproduction marks the work people do to support and expand powers for gendered self-determination that are put under threat. Queer social reproduction then refers to the work of making and sustaining networks, families, communities, and broader social paths through which queer people and comrades not only find, but *work* to create a broader set of gender freedom.[14] This means creating opportunities and cultures for both personal and collective resistance against dominant and dominating forms of gender socialization. This production and social reproduction of queer environments can vary in their aims from mere survival, to revolutionary struggle.[15] The upper limit of this queer social reproduction, as Alan Sears describes it, would be the "collective repossession" of the relations needed for "embodied freedom."[16]

While producing and reproducing communities that enable survival is necessary, it is not sufficient for socialist emancipation. Merely surviving is not living freely, nor is it a step towards living freely. Of course, without first finding ways to reproduce ourselves, our living personalities cannot flourish, and we can develop neither need-satisfying nor revolutionary powers. Strategically, SRT is politically committed to both the survival of oppressed people, and the collective, new organization of powers. Queer social reproduction is just one version of the many ways to organize and support each other, in the midst of oppression. In so doing, queer social reproduction shows that another way of organizing our powers is not only needed and possible, but valuable. Queer social reproduction means the organization of social reproduction through which all gender non-conforming and oppressed groups sustain their continued survival, and develop resistant capacities.[17] It is evidence of the power to move towards a more emancipated social organization.

Wherever SRT finds struggles to organize freer pathways, spaces, and communities for survival, the response to the *who* question can therefore be tied together with the response to the *what* question. Wherever the fight for survival is enjoined by alternative modes of social reproduction we see precisely where standard mechanisms for working class social reproduction are failing. Likewise, wherever oppressed people develop subcultures for their own social reproduction, powers for more complete liberation grow. For this reason, alternative modes of social reproduction also reveal where some of the greatest opportunities for radicalization towards socialist commitments are to be found.[18] Oppressed communities are growing powers that can be actualized in ways that instead of augmenting capital, and beyond merely surviving its devastations, can be turned back against it in struggle.[19]

Strategically this insight is important. Since class experiences are filtered through oppressions, the fight for survival in the midst of an oppressive society is always a fight that offers fertile ground for radical political developments. Overcoming oppression is not a sideshow which can be tidily isolated from class struggle. Social reproduction in the face of oppression develops the organizational skills, social relations, and openness to the critical insights and connective practices that can confront and overcome domination.[20]

The public education sector strike wave that started in early 2018 has provided ample evidence. Powers set in motion to provide better conditions for oneself can develop into broader socialist commitments.[21] The first step was to see striking and other forms of workplace action less as an action that "one" does and more as an action that a group or a "we" do together. Strikes are important radicalizing experiences because what may have been entered into as an attempt to secure better conditions for oneself, teaches individuals the necessity of solidarity with one's colleagues and community. In that way, strikes are valuable educators. Strikes teach working class people who their enemies are and what they are up against. They also teach people how to work together to develop and then actualize shared power for need-satisfaction rather than exclusively relying on oppression or exploitation-reproducing systems.

An anonymous teacher from Arizona provides forceful testimony of this experience. The teacher says: "please forgive me for being asleep my entire life," and insists that after their strike it would be impossible to "return to my previous slumber." Strikes can change horizons forever, and here the teacher is describing how the field of their social vision has been widened. The horizon of what matters and what appears possible has grown and, as a result, they are now committed to "fight for the many with little against the few with much." Struggle taught them to struggle more. SRT is strategically committed to struggles that will deepen and broaden working class commitments to fighting for socialism.

Developing socialism as a real possibility is a long-term commitment. The project requires political leaders who are willing to conceive of strikes over the long term as more than one-off industrial actions aimed at defending or advancing the interests of a particular firm's or school district's employees. While strikes can deepen a commitment to struggle, as we saw with the Arizonan teacher, they need to be developed into broader class militancy as well. The Vice President of the Chicago Teacher's Union, Stacy Davis-Gates, knew that this was the case. She adopted a social reproduction approach to striking when she tied Chicago teachers' readiness to strike to both the racism that deeply structures Chicago's public school system and the misogyny that diminishes the social recognition of women's work.

In many ways, Davis-Gates was following in the footsteps of her predecessors. Chicago teachers set the stage for both their 2019 strike and the tremendous growth in struggle in the education sector all across the US seven years earlier. In 2012, the same Chicago Teacher's Union, then led by Karen Lewis, staged a successful strike. Instead of resting on its laurels or merely extolling Lewis' excellent leadership, the union deepened its roots in its community. Sarah Jaffe writes that the Chicago Teacher's Union thought of itself as in:

> A fight to change politics in Chicago and in the country; it was big, and it was going to require allies. That meant figuring out a way to bring the community's issues to the bargaining table ... The union did that not by creating a cult of personality around the charismatic Lewis, but by delegating and distributing power and leadership across the union, spending money on an organizing department to make sure members were all involved in making decisions. It's an approach adopted by other reformers around the country, in places like Los Angeles, where the United Teachers Los Angeles successfully won its strike earlier this year. It's an approach that has rooted the union in neighborhoods around the city, with rank-and-file members working with the parents and students to make demands.[22]

This sustained connective work, going back many years, meant that most Chicagoans were already on the teachers' side when, in 2019, Davis-Gates tied the need to strike to the reality of under-supported schools: "students are told to grin and bear it because we do not find value in their communities." Because of this leg-work, supporting the teachers' strike could be easily seen as a kind of class-based community self-defense.[23] It is no surprise that charter schools joined the strike.[24]

Tying working class struggle to the forms of oppression and unmet needs experienced by communities is an essential part of SRT's political strategy. It is indeed the only way to combat the decomposition of the working class into individuals or its fragmentation into uncoordinated, competitive groups. SRT sees that the best way to grow powers for socialism is when labor struggles root themselves in the social reproduction of oppressed communities. By coordinating the answers to the *who* and the *what* questions, SRT promotes the strategic development of a socially integrated and solidarizing source for class struggle.

A socially integrated struggle that pays attention to oppressed groups is important in any era. But it's especially pressing today, as the far right continues to develop its forces. For the foreseeable future, capital-bolstering, left-silencing, scapegoating, and violence against the most disadvantaged of the working class will likely remain on the rise. The more capital produces isolated, atomized individuals, the more backlash against the material constraints inaugurated by capital will be channeled into the oppressions of racism, gender hierarchy and gender-binarism. Every violently ethno-nationalist, racist, and ableist response to the unmet needs of capitalist society is bonded together by the glue of violent gender commitments. This is because women and people whose very existence disrupts gender binarism pose an implicit challenge to the seamless unfolding of capitalist social relations.

Social reproductive work makes living personalities with robust needs and powers, and not just labor powers fit for valorizing capital. Queer social reproduction, for example, fashions whole communities that pose alternatives to the social relations, especially familial relations, most conducive to and problematically naturalized by capitalist arrangements. Both show us that there is and can be something more than capitalist exploitation and capitalist social relations. It is not that women and queer people are themselves revolutionary or can be substitutes for the proletariat. More than a few women and queer people are in fact quite conservative, and at least some are capitalists. Rather, the work done to reproduce living personalities and to build venues for non-conforming genders shows that we have needs as well as powers to develop a radically different society. Since these powers are so often constrained, there is great promise that they can be sharpened through struggle to pursue socialism, that is, the conditions through which they can be ever more freely developed.

Massive waves of popular mobilization against austerity, radicalizing feminist movements, worker solidarity across borders, the rise of self-defense organizations, pro-immigrant struggles at borders and ports of entry, confrontation with the police and immigration officers, the resurgence of Black radical energies and, of course, the return of the strike are all helping to bring this promise to light. Such mobilizations fight against dominating powers in ways that not only organize survival, but provide empowering lessons for further social struggle. In this way, they point to the growing possibility of socialism. It is not simply that since the crash of 2008 we can name "capitalism" as the problem, nor that "socialist" politicians are increasingly electable, and proud to declare their politics openly. It is also not that the far right again sees its enemy in what it often misconstrues as "Marxism." These are often merely linguistic developments, but they are also reflections of a deeper, changing reality.

Not only the language, but the skillful use of the strike is making a return. Massive mobilizations by workers are challenging the existing social and political order of things around the globe. In Haiti, Lebanon, Sudan, Chile, Ecuador, France, Uruguay, Iraq, Colombia, Iran, Mexico, Hong Kong, Argentina, the US and India we are witnessing a tremendous upsurge in radical potentials. SRT sees the hope for a new social order evolving out of this wave. And it provides a strategic view for how we can work to broaden and deepen class struggle. SRT's analysis and strategy sharpens revolutionary movements by helping working class people see their diverse powers—powers that can be set in motion not just despite, but ultimately to craft social forms *beyond* capitalist societies' violent constraints.

Postscript
Social Reproduction Theory
in and Beyond the Pandemic

COVID-19 has made our standard strategies for social reproduction entirely unreliable, and in doing so, has put the question to the very form of their organization. What I mean by "strategies for social reproduction" is simply the fact that there are always many different ways that we can organize the work we do to satisfy our needs. In the US and in most societies today, nearly everyone either has to work in exchange for a wage, or rely on those who do. We then use wages to pay, among other things, for our mortgage or rent, our food, transportation, outsourced care needs, and our debts.

In this society we produce and continuously reproduce our lives more or less as reliably as we can use them to generate wages. In the midst of the coronavirus pandemic, however, working in exchange for a wage has become impossible or deadly for many, and much more fraught with perils and stressful for everyone else. Those who depend on others' wages are even more vulnerable to the myriad, often gendered, forms of abuse that flow from relations of dependence.

Yet in this regime of social reproduction we can only satisfy our needs when paychecks come in. And this is why COVID-19 has put the question to forms of social reproduction that rely on exchanging our abilities to work for a wage. It is shining a light on and clarifying what was hidden or only dimly visible—that there is something troubling and violent in the way that we hang on the very possibility of waged work. And there is something deeply disturbing in how the wage and the work we are compelled to do for it dominates all our other needs and shapes, or better, contorts the way we reproduce ourselves. Now that the virus has equated working with taking increasing risks with one's life, the waged nature of reproducing life can start to seem like a bad bet.

It is not only that the virus has revealed a divided or even a fundamentally rotten society. While this is no doubt true, this insight was already well-prepared. The consequences of the crash and global recession of

2008 made class-based social analysis first possible and then increasingly popular. Who could have imagined back in 2005 that in just a decade, plausible candidates for executive office could again sound like social-democrats from previous generations.

Yet COVID-19 holds promise to push further. The virus has demonstrated to millions, and made millions more capable of seeing, the need for a fundamentally different organization of how we satisfy needs. Through the changed patterns of our daily lives, the virus has afforded a mental (if not for essential workers, a physical) distance from our standard way of abiding by and internalizing the capitalist mode of social reproduction. Through this distance, we are increasingly able to first see and then strongly object to the basic economic arrangements of the wage and capital's profit-driven arrangement of our social reproduction. To be sure, the virus has opened pathways for reactionary, authoritarian, and neo-fascist forms of rule, but it is also radicalizing our relationship to need in ways that can support far more hopeful politics.

Since SRT centers how we—as individuals, the working class, and society as a whole—produce and then maintain our need-satisfying capacities over time, it is also, as I've argued in this book, a theory that is committed to socialism. By socialism I simply mean to name the set of social relations through which we could most freely develop and use our capacities. In this view, SRT analyzes both the constraint of capitalist social relations and points to the possibilities for socialism beyond them. The way the COVID-19 pandemic has stemmed from but then disrupted capitalist social reproduction is ripe for SRT's analysis of constraints, while the way the pandemic has generated more radical commitments make the situation ripe for pursuing the socialism SRT points to.

Though there had been ample evidence that the way industry has been arranging production would likely sponsor similar viruses,[1] most did not heed the warnings. Agricultural and livestock production was arranged in facilities that were crowded to the point of danger for all involved. The close proximity of massive populations of different species of livestock increased the risk of viruses crossing and spreading between species. Finally, the extraordinarily interconnected nature of our social relations, combined with the speed with which we now traverse them has meant that viruses that previously died out before transmission are now capable of rapidly evolving in capitalist livestock production and then rapidly spreading from a small set of agricultural workers to billions of others.

A social reproduction view is helpful because the pandemic's con-sequences are in no sense naturally given. When our powers are constrained by a viral pandemic, SRT can show how the contours of that constraining mold are socially produced. Declining support for health-care and health-research has meant that adequate PPE and ventilators stock, as well as vaccines and ameliorative treatments were deemed insufficiently "necessary" or profitable to invest in. The risks we take in agricultural production were then magnified by the way states and localities, strapped for cash due to declining profitability of capital and thus tax revenues, turned to diminishing already precarious health infrastructure. Racist and classist disadvantages in inability to socially isolate and access health care were magnified, and the foreseeable result has finally happened: a viral pandemic is far more risky than necessary for all, and especially dangerous for those already most constrained by capitalist arrangements of social reproduction. Worse, the COVID-19 pandemic is just one instance of capitalist societies' tendencies to create self-induced crises of social reproduction, which will persist and deepen until a fundamentally different regime of social reproduction is in place.

SRT's twofold central insight is that our powers are beholden to capitalist economic pressures but also, and crucially, that they are the very tools through which capital gains its dominating force. With all but non-essential workers encouraged or forced to isolate as best they can, unemployment has increased, wages have declined, and in many instances, production has ground to a halt. The wages necessary for millions in the working class to reproduce themselves have fallen or been reduced to nothing. Even where economies have re-opened, economic production has diminished and we are all but assured of a deep reces-sion. For the most part our needs remain the same, but now and in the foreseeable future employment, and through it, our wage's ability to satisfy needs is diminished.

If, as I've argued, SRT sees that the pandemic-induced crisis of social reproduction is creating a crisis for capital but also the living person-alities and socially reproduced communities that provide it with labor power, what can it offer as a way out of this catastrophe? In other words, once renters see that they provide housing for landlords rather than the other way around, workers see that they need to and deserve to live, even when they cannot pay for necessities, and we all acknowledge the essen-tial work of social reproduction, what political ways forward can SRT point to? A helpful starting point is seeing how this burden and the experience of crisis is not borne equally by all.

In the midst of the ongoing pandemic SRT points to how different workers have tremendous burdens, but also different kinds of resistant powers. From nurses and teachers to Amazon warehouse workers we have seen how withholding embodied labor powers creates leverage that can be used to win safer conditions. When the already racist consequences of the pandemic combined with the ongoing pandemic of racist police violence, we witnessed the revitalization of #BLM in the largest protest movement in US history. As I've shown, SRT has fine resources to track not just exploitation of the working class, but the racist oppressions through which some in the working-class struggle, far too often, to simply live and then refashion the world in freer ways. The demand that Black lives indeed do and must matter, levelled over and against a society that is structurally organized around the opposite, highlights the need to make the liberation of our historically inflected living personalities and capacities the central commitment of socialist politics.

SRT can see how COVID-19 is magnifying the kinds of risks and sacrifices that different members of the working class are always forced to take. When we have to ask ourselves if we can afford to take a sick day, confront the police, risk arrest, or whether we can afford to pursue our needs for broader freedom when a constraining job is our path to health care or rent, the continued life of workers is posed against our ability to do what would be best for us. SRT is then committed to deepening and broadening the working class' recognition of their own powers within and ultimately against the capital-induced constraints we are pressured to accept. Through these powers, SRT envisions a socialist horizon beyond our need for wages and beyond our need to merely live through multiple pandemics or even one more day of drudgery. SRT's commitment to socialism promises a horizon in which our powers are socially produced and reproduced, quite simply for their own sake.

Notes

Websites last accessed April, 23, 2020.

INTRODUCTION: WHY THEORIZE SOCIAL REPRODUCTION?

1. www.youtube.com/watch?v=_cYpsDXXdHo at 48:14 and following.
2. A more expansive and complete historical reconstruction is available in Sue Ferguson's *Women and Work: Feminism, Labour, and Social Reproduction* (London: Pluto Press, 2019).
3. When I later refer to capital or capitalism as obeying this "imperative to valorize" this is what I mean.
4. See Tithi Bhattacharya's "Introduction" to *Social Reproduction Theory: Remapping Class, Recentering Oppression*, ed. Tithi Bhattacharya (London: Pluto Press, 2017).
5. See, for instance, K.D. Griffiths and J.J. Gleeson, "Kindercommunismus", https://subversionpress.files.wordpress.com/2015/06/kinderkom.pdf.
6. See, for instance, Sue Ferguson, "Children, Childhood and Capitalism: A Social Reproduction Perspective," in *Social Reproduction Theory: Remapping Class, Recentering Oppression*, ed. Tithi Bhattacharya (London: Pluto Press, 2017), pp. 112–30.
7. Throughout I will use "powers" and "capacities" interchangeably. Marx conflates labor powers (*Arbeitskraft*) with labor capacities (*Arbeitsvermögen*) and defines them as our mental and physical capabilities (*Fähigkeiten*) (see Chapter 2 n. 19).
8. Raya Dunayevskaya, interpreting Marx, was right to hold that "theory is not something the intellectual works out alone. Rather, the actions of the proletariat create the possibility for the intellectual to work out theory," in *Marxism and Freedom* (Amherst, NY: Humanity Books, 2000), p. 91.
9. Patricia Hill Collins, *Black Feminist Thought: Knowledge, Consciousness and the Politics of Empowerment*, 2nd edition (New York: Routledge, 2000), p. vi.

CHAPTER 1: SOCIAL REPRODUCTION THEORIES AS FRAMEWORKS FOR EMPIRICAL ANALYSIS

1. Nai, a pseudonym, was interviewed by International Women's Strike, New York City. Her full interview is available at www.publicseminar.org/2018/03/nai-new-immigrant-community-empowerment-nice/.
2. E. Marx and E. Aveling, "The Woman Question," available at www.marxists.org/archive/eleanor-marx/works/womanq.htm.

3. Bourgeois women's interests stem from their experiences as women and as members of the bourgeois class. Since bourgeois women largely managed households while proletarian women engaged with productive labor alongside the reproduction of embodied labor powers, what felt like constraints on the freedom of each, and therefore what the women's movement's aims ought to be, turned out to be quite different. Since class distinctions have remained, this division in the goals of the women's movement has likewise persisted. In the US it is also a deeply racialized division. See, for instance, Angela Davis, *Women, Race, and Class* (New York: Random House 1981).

4. August Bebel, *Woman and Socialism*, trans. Meta L. Stern (New York: The Co-Operative Press, 1910). For a discussion of Bebel, see Lise Vogel, *Marxism and the Oppression of Women: Towards a Unitary Theory* (Chicago: Haymarket, 2013) especially pp. 100–9.

5. Clara Zetkin, 1896, "Only in Conjunction with the Proletarian Woman Will Socialism Be Victorious," available at https://marxists.catbull.com/archive/zetkin/1896/10/women.htm.

6. Alexandra Kollontai, 1920, "Communism and the Family," available at www.marxists.org/archive/kollonta/1920/communism-family.htm. In this context "our" refers to Soviet society. The idea of a "triple oppression" was also developed by Claudia Jones to describe the unique burden of Black women. See Claudia Jones, "An End to the Neglect of the Problems of the Negro Woman!" in *Words on Fire: An Anthology of African-American Feminist Thought* (New York: The New Press, 1995), pp. 108–24.

7. Kollontai, "Communism and the Family."

8. Ibid.

9. Kollontai, 1921, "The Labour of Women in the Evolution of the Economy." Kollontai immediately acknowledged: "this principle is far from having been realised. In practice we lag behind our intentions." See www.marxists.org/archive/kollonta/1921/evolution.htm.

10. See Jones, "An End to the Neglect of the Problems of the Negro Woman!" p.120.

11. Leopoldina Fortunati, *The Arcane of Reproduction: Housework, Prostitution, Labor and Capital*, trans. Hilary Creek, ed. Jim Fleming (Brooklyn: Autonomedia, 1995), and Mariarosa Dalla Costa, "Women and the Subversion of the Community," in *Women and the Subversion of the Community: A Mariarosa Dalla Costa Reader*, ed. Camille Barbagallo (Oakland: PM Press, 2019), pp. 17–49. Fortunati now holds that things have been reversed and the sphere of reproduction dominates the sphere of production. See www.viewpointmag.com/2015/10/31/social-reproduction-but-not-as-we-know-it/. A similar position was arrived at decades earlier, in 1940, by Mary Inman. See "The Role of the Housewife in Social Production" republished by *Viewpoint Magazine*, available at www.viewpointmag.com/2015/10/31/the-role-of-the-housewife-in-social-production-1940/.

12. The heterosexual assumption would be challenged by Italian feminists but also by Marxists developing queer theory in a way that is consistent with, even if it does not use the exact terms of, social reproduction. See, for

instance, Sara Ahmed, whose "A Killjoy Survival Kit" at the end of *Living a Feminist Life* (Durham: Duke University Press, 2017) offers a queer, feminist, and radical approach to socially reproducing resistant communities.

13. See Mario Tronti, "Factory and Society," in *Workers and Capital*, trans. David Broder (London: Verso, 2019), pp. 12–35. See also Sylvia Federici's "Introduction," in *Revolution at Pointe Zero: Housework, Reproduction, and Feminist Struggle* (Oakland: PM Press, 2012), pp. 7–8.

14. In his drafts of *Capital*, Karl Marx himself warned against this strategy, arguing that simplifying a whole by negating the specific economic distinctions within it can offer only "a speculative approach." It would be better to conceive of the activities that do not produce value as conceptually distinguishable "moments," operating within a value-producing whole. Marx, *Grundrisse*, in *Marx-Engels Collected Works* vol. 28, p. 31. Hereafter the collected works will be cited as *MECW*.

15. These challenges will be developed in Chapter 4. Briefly, however, the naturalistic configuration of bodies tends to leave little space for gender non-conforming people, or at best attempts to accommodate them post hoc. By the same token, such naturalism can limit the revolutionary horizon with models of resistance that at best create some more space for freer ways of being a woman, but leave capitalism relatively unchallenged.

16. For instance, there are, at the time of writing, nearly 650,000 views of the "Witchcraft, Gender, and Marxism" video by PhilosophyTube on youtube. com (www.youtube.com/watch?v=tmk47kh7fiE) which, in the first half, prominently features Federici's analysis of witch-hunts.

17. Even when such a movement was declining or at a lull, the theory was kept alive by the work, in particular, of Sue Ferguson, Martha Gimenez, Cindi Katz, and Johanna Brenner and Barbara Laslett. Each refined categories and developed their own concrete social analyses. Likewise, quite a few anthropologists developed the kinds of empirical studies that Lise Vogel insisted was needed to flesh out a social reproduction understanding of women's oppression under conditions of capital.

18. There have been special issues devoted to SRT in *Viewpoint Magazine*, www.viewpointmag.com/2015/11/02/issue-5-social-reproduction/, *Radical Philosophy*, 2.04 (Spring, 2019), *Historical Materialism* 24:2 (June, 2016), *Capital & Class* 43:4 (December, 2019), and *Comparative Literature and Culture* (June, 2020). See also Bhattacharya, *Social Reproduction Theory*.

19. Marx makes the argument in the *Grundrisse* by contrasting the value-productive work of making a piano with the socially valuable but not economically "productive" work of playing it. See *MECW* vol. 28, p. 231. Even if playing the piano for resting workers, for instance, really helped regenerate their powers to work, this playing itself would not be value-productive.

20. Marx recognized the ecological point in the first volume of *Capital* when holding that "Capitalist production ... develops technology, and the combining together of various processes into a social whole, only by sapping the original sources of all wealth—the soil and the labourer," *MECW* vol. 35, p. 508.

21. Thinking the guiding force of capital as a "heartbeat" is suggested by the way Marx describes capital pumping surplus-value out of labor in *Capital* vol. 1 at *MECW* vol. 35, p. 314, p. 426 and, especially in vol. 3 at *MECW* 37, pp. 777–8. The latter provides core textual support for SRT's ability to appreciate how surplus-value is "pumped" out of producers across different relations of production. In "Remarks on Gender," Cinzia Arruzza developed the necessity as well as the limits of appreciating the valorizing "heart" of capitalism: "to try to explain what capitalist society is only in terms of surplus-value extraction is like trying to explain the anatomy of the human body by explaining only how the heart works." See "Remarks on Gender," *Viewpoint Magazine*, available at www.viewpointmag.com/2014/09/02/ remarks-on-gender/. This way of thinking will be further explored in Chapter 4.

22. At least obliquely, Marx seems to agree with this view when he writes, in *Capital* vol. 1, "we assume that the capitalist sells at their value the commodities he has produced, without concerning ourselves either about the new form that capital assumes while in the sphere of circulation, or about the concrete conditions of reproduction hidden under these forms … We, therefore, first of all consider accumulation from an abstract point of view." *MECW* vol. 35, p. 565.

23. See especially Bhattacharya, "Introduction."

24. It does not follow, however, that the creation and the daily work of disciplining and regenerating tired out labor powers itself valorizes capital unless, of course, this regenerative work is done for profit. This crucial distinction is sometimes blurred by social reproduction theorists. See, for instance, Alessandra Mezzadri, "On the Value of Social Reproduction," *Radical Philosophy* 2.04 (Spring, 2019), available at www.radicalphilosophy. com/article/on-the-value-of-social-reproduction. Mezzadri conflates labor control, externalizing the costs of reproducing labor, and ongoing formal subsumption, the effect of which contribute to the production of value, with "direct" value production itself. Not marking distinctions between value production and other activities or policies that enable or speed up value production has the effect of blurring what "value" itself refers to.

25. Howard Botwinick provides a fine starting point to move in this direction in *Persistent Inequalities* (Chicago: Haymarket, 2018).

26. The endnotes collective makes this point quite clear in "The Logic of Gender on the Separation of Spheres and the Logic of Abjection," *Endnotes* 3, available at https://endnotes.org.uk/issues/3/en/endnotes-the-logic-of-gender.

27. Some theorists of social reproduction have sought to expand the notion of value to encompass socially reproductive work. Considering such work unwaged and feminized is, for instance, the path taken by Fortunati in her seminal *The Arcane of Reproduction* as well as Dalla Costa, *Women and the Subversion of the Community*. I consider these efforts unconvincing. See especially, Paul Smith, "Domestic Labour and Marx's Theory of Value," in *Feminism and Materialism: Women and Modes of Production*, eds. Annette

Kuhn and Annmarie Wolpe (London: Routledge and Kegan Paul, 1978), pp. 198–219.

28. It would be possible to provide an account of the social reproduction of non-capitalist societies as well, but doing so would require using an entirely different notion of "value."

29. A full transcript and video of Le Guin's speech is available at www.sfcenter. ku.edu/LeGuin-NBA-Medalist-Speech.htm.

30. Marx, *Capital* vol. 1, *MECW* vol. 35, p. 565.

31. Marx developed exactly this point in *Theories of Surplus Values:* "capital itself regulates this production of labour power, the production of the mass of human beings it intends to exploit, in accordance with its requirements for this exploitation. Capital therefore does not just produce capital, it produces a growing mass of workers, the material which alone enables it to function as additional capital. Hence not only does labour produce the conditions of labour on an ever increasing scale as capital, in opposition to itself; capital, for its part, produces on an ever increasing scale the productive wage labourers it requires. Labour produces its conditions of production as capital, and capital produces labour as the means of its realization as capital, as wage labour. Capitalist production is not only the reproduction of the relation, it is its reproduction on an ever growing scale; and in the same proportion as the social productive power of labour develops, along with the capitalist mode of production, the pile of wealth confronting the worker grows, as wealth ruling over him, as capital, and the world of wealth expands vis-à-vis the worker as an alien and dominating world." See *MECW* vol. 34, p. 463.

32. Cinzia Arruzza makes this point in showing how a social reproduction view can think of the economy not only as an abstract necessitating logic, but "as a set of living social relations." See "Functionalist, Determinist, Reductionist: Social Reproduction Feminism and its Critics," *Science & Society* 80:1 (2016), pp. 9–30, p. 25.

33. See, for instance, the detailed work done from social reproduction vantage points in *Social Reproduction: Feminist Political Economy Challenges Neoliberalism*, eds. Kate Bezanson and Meg Luxton (Montreal: McGill-Queen's University Press, 2006).

34. For instance, Antonella Picchio highlights the gendered reproduction of labour power through an economic analysis that traces the blind-spots of liberal economic methods. See *Social Reproduction: The Political Economy of the Labor Market* (Cambridge: Cambridge University Press, 1992).

35. Cindi Katz's exploration of the "geography" of social reproduction and the use of "topography" to analyze its harms and shared political responses is helpful here. For the former, see Katz, "Vagabond Capitalism and the Necessity of Social Reproduction," *Antipode*, 33 (2001), pp. 709–28, and the latter Katz, "On the Grounds of Globalization: A Topography for Feminist Political Engagement," *Signs* (2001), 26:4, pp. 1213–34.

36. See, for instance, Sue Ferguson, "Canadian Contributions to Social Repro-
    duction Feminism, Race and Embodied Labour," *Race, Gender & Class*, 15:
    1–2 (2008), pp. 42–57.
37. See US Bureau of Labor Statistics' Injuries, Illnesses, and Fatalities report,
    Table R38, "Number of nonfatal occupational injuries and illnesses involv-
    ing days away from work by industry and race or ethnic origin of worker,
    private industry, 2017," available at www.bls.gov/iif/oshwc/osh/case/cd_
    r38_2017.htm.
38. Sara Farris uses SRT at precisely this conjuncture to provide superior
    analysis. See "Social Reproduction and Racialized Surplus Populations"
    in *Capitalism: Concept, Idea, Image – Aspects of Marx's Capital Today*, eds.
    P. Osborne; É. Alliez and E.-J. Russell, (Kingston upon Thames: CRMEP,
    2019) pp. 121–31.
39. See, for instance, Ferguson, *Women and Work*. For the project of a socially
    situated life-making oriented towards freedom over and against the logics of
    its constraint. See also Mariana Mora's *Kuxlejal Politics* (Austin: University
    of Texas, 2017).
40. See, for instance, Sophie Lewis' *Full Surrogacy Now: Feminist Against Family*
    (London: Verso, 2019) for one compelling way to develop the individual and
    social dimension of the inter-generational sense of life-making.

CHAPTER 2: POWER AS POTENTIALITY OR
THE CRITICAL DIMENSION OF LABOR POWER

1. Ana, a pseudonym, was interviewed by International Women's Strike, New
   York City. Her full interview is available at www.publicseminar.org/2017/05/
   testimony-ana/.
2. For a fine analysis of how and why this mental production of masculinity is continuously available despite it being deeply outmoded, see Norbert
   Trenkle, "The Rise and Fall of the Working Man: Toward a Critique of
   Modern Masculinity," in *Marxism and the Critique of Value*, eds. N. Larsen,
   M. Nilges, J. Robinson, and N. Brown (Chicago: MCM Publishing, 2014),
   pp. 145–9.
3. Marx, *Capital* vol. 1, *MECW* vol. 35, p. 177. Marx here conflates labor
   powers and labor capacities. Since "capacity" is how Marx qualified the
   potential for labor in the *Grundrisse*, the definition linking the two together
   here permits me to draw on accounts of labor capacity Marx developed not
   just in *Capital* but in the *Grundrisse* as well.
4. This approach follows the interpretive footsteps of Sue Ferguson, who also
   works with a broad notion of labor power. See Ferguson, "Canadian Contributions to Social Reproduction Feminism," p. 49.
5. Marx, *Capital* vol. 1, *MECW* vol. 35, p. 196.
6. Ibid., p. 194.
7. Ibid., p. 178.
8. Ibid., p. 70.

9. See, for instance, Jason Read, *The Micro-Politics of Capital: Marx and the Prehistory of the Present* (Albany: SUNY Press, 2003), p. 136.

10. Alexey Stakhanov was hailed for breaking mining records and widely publicized as the epitome of the Soviet Union's tireless worker.

11. See *Capital* vol. 2, *MECW* vol. 36, p. 402.

12. According to historian E.P. Thompson, there were very significant changes in the social expectations for diet and drink in different parts of the English working classes in just the first half of the nineteenth century. See *The Making of the English Working Class* (New York: Vintage Books, 1966), pp. 314 ff.

13. In what follows I draw loosely on work by György Márkus in his excellent *Marxism and Anthropology: The Concept of "Human Essence" in the Philosophy of Marx* (Sydney: modem-Verlag, 2014).

14. See Marx, *Grundrisse*, *MECW* vol. 28, p. 530 where Marx defines real freedom as the freedom to self-realize through the work of need-satisfying activity. Marx is careful to show that the social conditions for work will have a lot to say in determining if work will actually be a process of self-realization.

15. This is not to say that all of our needs are equally valid. The capitalist's need to valorize is a socially produced need just as much as the worker's need to freely develop and realize her capacities. That one need (the capitalist's) is more realizable given the logic put into place by a society with property relations that divides people into bosses and workers does not change the fact that all of us are needy beings, and our social position highly influences our needs. See Ágnes Heller, *The Theory of Needs in Marx* (London: Allison and Busby, 1976).

16. For Marx, see, for instance, the description of the need for socialization as a means to self-reproduction as well as the radical need for the strength of social bonds themselves in the *Economic and Philosophic Manuscripts of 1844* in *MECW* vol. 3, p. 313.

17. See, for instance, Anwar Shaikh, *Capitalism: Competition, Crisis* (Oxford: Oxford University Press, 2016). Kate Doyle Griffiths is the first, to my knowledge, to use the expression "crisis of care" to refer to the decidedly unstable ways labor powers are reproduced under conditions of capital in South Africa. "Social Reproduction and South Africa's Precarious Politics," for the panel Gender and Social Reproduction at the Historical Materialism Conference, SOAS, London, November 7–10. Nancy Fraser has since used the term in more general ways. The notion of a "crisis" of social reproduction, and the racial aspects of such a crisis, has been developed by Jasmine Gibson, "Fire This Time: Notes on the Crisis of Reproduction," *Lies Journal* 2 (2015), pp. 143–55, available at www.liesjournal.net/volume2.pdf.

18. See Aaron Jaffe, "From Aristotle to Marx: A Critical Philosophical Anthropology," *Science & Society* 80 (2016), pp. 56–77.

19. *Capital* vol. 1, *MECW* vol. 35, p. 572. This *MECW* translation suffers from a few problems. There is no need to translate "eines Menschen" in a gendered way with "he" as the text does. Unlike the Fowkes translation available in the

Penguin editions of *Capital* vol. 1, this translation very unfortunately leaves entirely untranslated Marx's stress on corporeality and living personality in the definition of labor powers. In the German edition, labor powers and capacities exist in our living corporality: "*Unter Arbeitskraft oder Arbeitsvermögen verstehen wir den Inbegriff der physischen und geistigen Fähigkeiten, die in der Leiblichkeit, der lebendigen Persönlichkeit eines Menschen existieren ...*" (emphasis added). In the French edition, which Marx personally approved, this stress on living embodiment is equally clear: "*Sous ce nom [puissance de travail ou force de travail] il faut comprendre l'ensemble des facultés physiques et intellectuelles qui existent dans le corps d'un homme, dans sa personnalité vivante ...*" (emphasis added). Marx did not have "labor power" as a central category when writing the *German Ideology*. However, he developed a very similar thought, tying the conditions of our activity to our production and reproduction in this early work as well: "This mode of production must not be considered simply as being the reproduction of the physical existence of the individuals. Rather it is a definite form of activity of these individuals, a definite form of expressing their life, a definite mode of life on their part. As individuals express their life, so they are. What they are, therefore, coincides with their production, both with what they produce and with how they produce. Hence what individuals are depends on the material conditions of their production." *MECW* vol. 5, pp. 31–2.

20. Sandro Chignola offers a conceptually sensitive and careful account of Marx's labor powers as embodied in a lively way, through living personalities in "Body Factories," in *Thinking the Body as a Basis, Provocation and Burden of Life*, eds. Gert Melville and Carlos Ruta (Berlin: De Gruyter, 2015), pp. 3–18.

21. Marx, *Capital* vol. 1, *MECW* vol. 35, p. 204.

22. Isabella Bakker and Stephen Gill make a similar point when insisting that their ontology—or theory of being—is one of continuously "transformative *process*." See "Ontology, Method, and Hypotheses," in *Power, Production and Social Reproduction: Human In/Security in the Global Political Economy*, eds. Isabella Bakker and Stephen Gill (London: Palgrave Macmillan, 2003), p. 18.

23. This approach can criticize capitalist societies as well as non-capitalist ones. The critical approach developed here will not be terribly satisfying to those who oppose thinking the human as such, or think that any account of the human is itself necessarily violent.

24. The following, therefore, tries to make good on Himani Bannerji's thought that the "task of social theory requires that it be able to discover the mediations of different social moments in non-polar terms, and bring out the 'specificity' of any fragment of experience by providing it with a general name as well as with a particular authenticity at the same time. That is, it must show how any situation/experience is distinctively, particularly, locally itself and yet/also constituted by and exemplary of social forces which lie in, around and beyond it." See "But Who Speaks For Us? Experience and

Agency in Conventional Feminist Paradigms," in *Unsettling Relations: The University as a Site of Feminist Struggles* (Boston: South End Press, 1992), pp. 67–107, p. 78. My reconstruction of SRT joins Bannerji in rejecting merely economistic approaches to the criticism of capital.

25. For a methodological development of this commitment, see D. McNally, "The Dialectics of Unity and Difference in the Constitution of Wage-Labour," *Capital & Class* 39:1 (2015), pp. 131–46.

26. This is precisely what is signaled in the subtitle of T. Bhattacharya's edited volume, *Remapping Class, Recentering Oppression*. Bhattacharya's "Introduction" finely develops this commitment.

27. This is why versions of SRT that see the violence of capital as constraining human labor powers to means of valorization are not wrong, but are too narrow. See, for instance, Bakker and Gill's not entirely accurate reinterpretation of Sue Ferguson (in "Building on the Strengths of the Socialist Feminist Tradition," *Critical Sociology* 25:1 (1999), pp. 1–15): "the social and power relations of capital reduced the creative capacities and potentials of workers to an instrumentality, with the effect that it transformed the advantages of human freedom and its objectification into means to accumulate profit," in Isabella Bakker and Stephen Gill, *Power, Production, and Social Reproduction*, p. 21. Isabella Bakker and Rachel Silvey offer a broader view of capital's harm in the "Introduction" to their *Beyond States and Markets: The Challenges of Social Reproduction* (London: Routledge, 2008), p. 3.

28. See, for instance, Randolph B. Persaud, "Power, Production, and Racialization in Global Labor Recruitment and Supply," in *Power, Production, and Social Reproduction*, eds. Isabella Bakker and Stephen Gill (London: Palgrave Macmillan, 2003), pp. 124–45.

29. As David Camfield notes, working with this broad notion of labor means gender oppression, as well as other forms of oppression are not merely "added-on." Instead they are internally connected to and parts of our criticism of capital. See his "Beyond Adding on Gender and Class: Revisiting Marxism and Feminism," *Studies in Political Economy* 68:1 (2002), pp. 37–54.

CHAPTER 3: THE QUESTION OF IMMANENCE
AND THE SOCIAL FORM OF LABOR POWER

1. Alicia, a pseudonym, was interviewed by International Women's Strike, New York City. Her full interview is available at www.publicseminar.org/2018/03/alicia-golden-steps/.

2. Marx, *Capital* vol. 1, *MECW* vol. 35, p. 188.

3. It is also the case that ideologies can constrain our freedom. It is often de-capacitating to blindly identify with oppressive structures, to see them but think that things can't be otherwise, or to defer hopes for liberation to an indefinite beyond (or afterlife). While it is beyond the scope of this chapter, SRT's commitment to expanding the freedom of our powers is also well

suited to integrate analysis and criticism of how these and other ideologies are produced and reproduced. Louis Althusser moves in this direction in *On the Reproduction of Capitalism: Ideology and Ideological State Apparatuses*, trans. G.M. Goshgarian (London: Verso, 2014).

4. That it tokens a better alternative means neither that individual instances in the midst of capitalism are sustainable in the long term, nor that building such cooperative enterprises is the single or best way to pursue freer social arrangements.

5. Developing the critical thrust of this idea, Marx holds that capital does create abstract and homogeneous labor: capital's "general value form is the reduction of all kinds of actual labour to their common character of being human labour generally, of being the expenditure of human labour power." *Capital* vol. 1, *MECW* vol. 35, p. 78. Marx's point here is that capital relies on and reproduces a tremendous amount of specialized and thus quite specific capacities to labor while determining their *value* in an abstract, one-size-fits-all way.

6. See, for instance, Martha Gimenez, "The Dialectics of Waged and Unwaged Work: Waged Work, Domestic Labour and Household Survival in the United States," in *Marx, Women, and Capitalist Social Reproduction* (Leiden: Brill, 2019), pp. 234–56.

7. The relational freedom offered by SRT can therefore be understood as an ongoing attempt to escape absolute domination, and can be compared to the rich description of freedom in Neil Robert's *Freedom as Marronage* (Chicago: Chicago University Press, 2015). Yet, beyond Robert's upper political limit, described at the end of his book as merely a "taming of the Leviathan," SRT can throw into question the relations that constrain freedom to such taming or only fleeting moments of escape. Like Walter Rodney's more revolutionary inheritance of Black Caribbean movements, it offers a wider revolutionary horizon, which I develop in Chapter 6. See, for instance, Rodney's "The Groundings with My Brothers," in the collected volume *The Groundings with My Brothers* (London: Bogle-L'Ouverture Publications, 1969), pp. 59–67.

8. Dalla Costa applies this approach in her analysis of the changing conditions through which women reproduced labor power in *Family Welfare and the State: Between Progressivism and the New Deal*, trans. Rafaella Capanna (Brooklyn: Common Notions, 2015).

9. Jean Baudrillard offers a powerful criticism of such a "productive" way of seeing things in *The Mirror of Production*, trans. Mark Poster (New York: Telos Press, 1975), but SRT, as it is developed in what follows, shows that using this criticism as wholesale rejection of Marxism is unwarranted.

10. I want to thank Rosa Patterson for helping to recognize the danger of a framework that naively imports valuation of "power" and "capacity" without challenging how what counts as powers and capacities are themselves socially determined in harmful ways. In what follows I am close to the social model of disability. This view divides impairment from disability,

arguing that we are disabled by our society's (mis)treatment of those with impairments.

11. Richard Jenkins, "Disability and Social Stratification," *The British Journal of Sociology* 42:4 (1991), pp. 557–80. British disability activists often use the term "disabilism" where US activists would use "ableism" to suggest the origins of disability in society's response to impairment. I depart from Jenkins' accounts of class and believe that a social reproduction frame can respond to much of his resistance to class analysis. I am particularly interested in the way Garland-Thomson describes a "misfit" as the disjunction between "bodies with particular shapes and capabilities," on the one hand, and "the particular shape and structure of the world," but would analytically center capitalism as a key component structuring the world. See "Misfits: A Feminist Materialist Disability Concept," *Hypatia* 26:3 (2011), pp. 591–609, p. 594. Such a view is developed in Russell and Malhotra, "Capitalism and Disability," in *Socialist Register 2002*, eds. L. Panitch and C. Leys (London: Merlin Press, 2001), pp. 211–28.

12. It is no accident that the US federal Office of Disability Employment Policy has had its budget cut from over $38 to just $27 million for fiscal year 2020. Diminishing the already scant social resources that help activate powers in an employable way further naturalizes disability.

13. Marx, *Critique of the Gotha Voting Program, MECW* vol. 24, p. 87.

14. Ibid., p. 87.

15. Ibid., p. 86.

16. See Amy De'Ath, "Gender and Social Reproduction," in *The Sage Handbook of Frankfurt School Critical Theory*, eds. B. Best, W. Bonefeld, and C. O'Kane (London, Sage: 2018), pp. 1534–50. See also Aaron Jaffe "Social Reproduction Theory and the Form of Labor Power" *Comparative Literature and Culture* 22:2 (2020).

CHAPTER 4: THE BODY AND GENDER
IN SOCIAL REPRODUCTION THEORY

1. Alyssa's interview with New York City's Trans Oral History Project is available in full at https://s3.amazonaws.com/oral-history/transcripts/NYC+TOHP+Transcript+073+Alyssa+Pariah.pdf. The transcript has been slightly edited for spelling.

2. Silvia Federici, *Caliban and the Witch* (New York: Autonomedia, 2004), p. 141. This manuscript was prepared prior to being able to access Federici's *The Periphery of the Skin* (Oakland: PM Press, 2020).

3. Federici, *Caliban and the Witch*, p. 152.

4. This is perhaps what motivates Federici to tell a rather one-size-fits-all story about women's oppression in wide-ranging transitions to capitalism.

5. See both "The Reproduction of Labor Power in the Global Economy and the Unfinished Feminist Revolution," p. 111 and "Women, Land Struggles, and Globalization: An International Perspective," pp. 131 ff., in Silvia Federici,

Revolution at Point Zero: Housework, Reproduction, and Feminist Struggle (Oakland: PM Press, 2012).

6. See Jasbir K. Puar's *The Right to Maim* (Durham: Duke University Press, 2017) for an account that links existing forms of trans inclusion to the normative logic of violently disabling state, medical, and capital-driven regimes.

7. I follow Kay Gabriel in thinking gender through embodied, relationally configured desires that are immersed within capitalist political economy. See "Gender as Accumulation Strategy," *Invert Journal*. Available at https://invertjournal.org.uk/posts?view=articles&post=7106265#gender-as-accumulation-strategy.

8. See Nat Raha, "Transfeminine Brokennness, Radical Feminism," *South Atlantic Quarterly* 116:3 (2017), pp. 632–46. Also, Holly Lewis, *The Politics of Everybody: Feminism, Queer Theory, and Marxism at the Intersection* (London: Zed Books, 2016).

9. See Michelle O'Brien's review "Queer in the Eras of Capital" of Peter Drucker, *Warped: Gay Normality and Queer Anticapitalism* at H-Socialism, available at https://networks.h-net.org/node/11717/reviews/191679/obrien-drucker-warped-gay-normality-and-queer-anti-capitalism, Jules Gleeson's "Transition and Abolition: Notes on Marxist and Trans Practice," available at www.viewpointmag.com/2017/07/19/transition-and-abolition-notes-on-marxism-and-trans-politics/ as well as "An Aviary of Queer Social Reproduction," *Hypocrite Reader* 94 (2019), available at http://hypocrite reader.com/94/eggs-queer-social-reproduction. See also Noah Zazanis' talk for the "The Queer Psyche under Capitalism" panel of the Socialism in Our Time Conference, Saturday, April 13, 2019.

10. See, respectively, Vogel, *Marxism and the Oppression of Women*, p. 135, p. 140, and p. 154.

11. Ibid., p. 139.

12. See Lewis, *Full Surrogacy Now*.

13. Vogel, *Marxism and the Oppression of Woman*, p. 147.

14. At the time, and drawing on de Beauvoir, Monique Wittig was making steps in this direction. See "The Category of Sex" and "One Is Not Born a Woman" in the collected volume *The Straight Mind and Other Essays* (Boston: Beacon Press, 1992, pp. 1–8 and 9–20).

15. For a criticism of the general tendency in Marxist feminism to reduce women's oppression to a biologically reproductive basis, see Stevi Jackson, "Marxism and Feminism," in *Marxism and Social Science*, eds. A. Gamble, D. Marsh, and T. Tant (London: Macmillan, 1999), pp. 11–34.

16. Johanna Brenner and Maria Ramas, "Rethinking Women's Oppression," *New Left Review* 1/144 (1984), pp. 33–71, pp. 47–8. For further explanations for why SRT need not be biologically reductive in accepting this mode of explanation, see also Arruzza, "Functionalist, Determinist, Reductionist" and M. Gimenez, "Capitalism and the Oppression of Women: Marx Revisited," *Science & Society* 69:1 (2005), pp. 11–32.

17. The way Dalla Costa describes the deep constraints on women's capacities in "Women and the Subversion of the Community" can be expanded to

include the gender-normative effects of the nuclear family as well. There are moves in this direction in the discussion of imposed femininity and the constraints on women's sexuality. "Women and the Subversion of the Community," in *Women and the Subversion of Community: A Mariarosa Dalla Costa Reader*, ed. Camille Barbagallo, trans. Richard Braude (Oakland: PM Press, 2019), pp. 17–49.

18. See, for instance, the suggested line of development in Sébastien Rioux, "Embodied Contradictions: Capitalism, Social Reproduction, and Body Formation," *Women's Studies International Forum* 48 (2015), pp. 194–202.

CHAPTER 5: REPRODUCING INTERSECTIONS AND SOCIAL REPRODUCTION

1. Cynthia was interviewed by International Women's Strike, New York City. Her full interview is available at www.publicseminar.org/2018/03/cynthia-brandworkers/.

2. Sojourner Truth, "Ain't I a Woman." The transcription by Marius Robinson shortly after Truth's speech is considered more accurate than the better-known version by Frances Gage from 1863. For access to both, see www.thesojournertruthproject.com/compare-the-speeches.

3. W.E.B. Du Bois, *Black Reconstruction* (Oxford: Oxford University Press, 2007).

4. For a brief reconstruction of the history and trajectories of the theories, see https://mronline.org/2012/04/12/aguilar120412-html/. For a more complete reconstruction, see Ashley Bohrer, *Marxism and Intersectionality: Race, Gender, Class, and Sexuality under Contemporary Capitalism* (Beilefeld: Transcript Verlag, 2019).

5. See the Combahee River Collective, "A Black Feminist Perspective," in *This Bridge Called My Back*, eds. Cherrie Moraga and Gloria Anzaldúa (Albany: SUNY Press, 2015), pp. 210–18.

6. Sara Salem, "Intersectionality and its Discontents: Intersectionality as Travelling Theory. A Marxist Feminist Critique," *European Journal of Women's Studies* 2:4, pp. 403–18. Intersectionality's malleability has made it capable of fitting the theoretical needs of feminists around the world. Although in what follows my reconstruction focuses on Patricia Hill Collins, I find it valuable that Collins' work emphasizes both the theories' wide use and applicability, as well as the US-specific conditions she is deeply concerned with.

7. For "Oppression Olympics," see Elizabeth Martínez, *De Colores Means All of Us: Latina Views for a Multi-Colored Century* (Cambridge, MA: South End Press, 1998). For the commitment to fighting, see the influential collection *This Bridge Called My Back*, eds. Cherríe Moraga and Gloria Anzaldúa (Albany: SUNY Press, 2015).

8. "Misogynoir" has been used to describe the particular harms suffered by Black women. See Moya Bailey, who coined the term, and Trudy in their

discussion "On Misogynoir: Citation, Erasure, and Plagiarism," *Feminist Media Studies* 18 (2018), pp. 762–8. "Transmisogynoir" further specifies the harm by singling out the forms most suffered by Black trans women. Trudy seems to be have coined the term in a tweet @thetrudz 9:35 pm, August 14, 2013.

9. Collins, *Black Feminist Thought*.
10. Ibid., p. 18 (emphasis added).
11. Ibid., p. 23 and p. 127.
12. Ibid., p. 131, as well as pp. 276 ff.
13. Ibid., p. 228.
14. Ibid., p. 231.
15. Ibid., p. 287.
16. Ibid., p. 275.
17. In a more extensive reconstruction this would be the point to bring in María Lugones' developments of resistant "mestiza consciousness" in "On *Borderlands/La Frontera*: An Interpretive Essay," *Hypatia* 7:4 (1992), pp. 31–7. The concept of "enmeshed" oppressions also provides a way to more concretely ground the experience abstractly thought in a "matrix." See Lugones' *Pilgrimages/Peregrinajes: Theorizing Coalition Against Multiple Oppressions* (Lanham: Rowman and Littlefield, 2003), especially pp. 207 ff.
18. Collins, *Black Feminist Thought*, pp. 273–4.
19. Ibid., p. 270.
20. Martha Gimenez, "Intersectionality," *Science & Society* 82:2 (2018), pp. 261–9, p. 263.
21. Martha Gimenez, "Reflections on Intersectionality," in *Marx, Women, and Capitalist Social Reproduction* (Leiden: Brill, 2019), pp. 94–109, p. 108 (emphasis in original).
22. Ashley Bohrer, "Intersectionality and Marxism: A Critical Historiography," *Historical Materialism* 26:2 (2018), pp. 46–74, p. 64.
23. See Ferguson, "Intersectionality and Social-Reproduction Feminisms," *Historical Materialism* 24:2 (2016), pp. 38–60.
24. Tithi Bhattacharya, for instance, criticizes intersectionality as a theory, but maintains that most people identifying as intersectional feminists are signaling a commitment to anti-racism, and for this reason social reproduction feminists can and should work with them. I agree. See her interview at www.rs21.org.uk/2017/12/21/capitalisms-life-source-the-domestic-and-social-basis-for-exploitation/.
25. Collins, *Black Feminist Thought*, p. 270.
26. See, for instance, Ellen Meiksins Wood, "Capitalism and Human Emancipation," *New Left Review* I/88 (1988), pp. 3–20.
27. Eve Mitchell, for instance, develops this "ahistorical" charge in "I Am a Woman and a Human: A Marxist-Feminist Critique of Intersectionality Theory," at www.unityandstruggle.org/2013/09/i-am-a-woman-and-a-human-a-marxist-feminist-critique-of-intersectionality-theory/. Since Mitchell sees the categories as ahistorical, she reads the identities that flow from intersectionality as one-sided, constrained forms of life-activity. While agreeing

with Mitchell that naturalized identities are often reproduced as alienated moments of a totality, the best versions of intersectionality are compatible with Marxism's more general view of a historical totality that unfolds through its moments of alienation.

28. Rosemary Hennessy, in *Profit and Pleasure: Sexual Identities in Late Capitalism* (New York: Routledge, 2000), p. 22 and pp. 215 ff. provides an excellent account of how a mode of production outlaws some needs. This approach is particularly valuable for queer versions of social reproduction. I follow Hennessy more generally in using class-analysis to think through the social possibilities of and constraints on desire.

29. See, for instance, Walter Rodney, *How Europe Underdeveloped Africa* (London: Verso, 2018). Mai Taha and Sara Salem develop a valuable intersectional version of SRT appropriate to the "post-colonial moment" in "Social Reproduction and Empire in an Egyptian Century," *Radical Philosophy* 2.04 (2019), available at www.radicalphilosophy.com/article/social-reproduction-and-empire-in-an-egyptian-century.

30. See, for instance, Stephen Resnick and Richard Wolff, *Knowledge and Class* (Chicago: University of Chicago Press, 1987), pp. 115ff. and pp. 159–60.

31. Marx describes how the introduction of machinery intensifies the working process, and exacerbates and reproduces already given differences. See *Capital* vol. 1, *MECW* vol. 35, p. 354.

32. Responding to the worrying thought that the most we could ever offer are provincial accounts of capital, Vivek Chibber developed an approach similar to that offered here. In *Postcolonial Theory and the Specter of Capital* (London: Verso, 2013, p. 111) he acknowledges differing relations of domination but holds that "what capitalism universalizes … is a particular strategy of economic reproduction. It compels economic units to focus single-mindedly on accumulating ever more capital."

33. For a forceful version of this argument, see Lewis, *The Politics of Everybody*, pp. 192–5.

34. Marx, *Capital* vol. 3, *MECW* vol. 37, pp. 777–8.

35. See, for instance, Etienne Balibar's contribution to *Reading Capital*, trans. Ben Brewster (London: Verso, 1979), p. 220 and following. See also Stuart Hall, "Race, Articulation and Societies Structured in Dominance," *Essential Writings of Stuart Hall* vol. 1, ed. David Morley (Durham: Duke University Press, 2019), pp. 172–221.

36. Marx, *Grundrisse, MECW* vol. 29, p. 210. The idea that we reproduce our lives through highly specific and individuated contributions to a given mode of production is also forcefully made by Marx in the *German Ideology*: a "mode of production must not be considered simply as being the reproduction of the physical existence of the individuals. Rather it is a definite form of activity of these individuals, a definite form of expressing their life, a definite mode of life on their part. As individuals express their life, so they are. What they are, therefore, coincides with their production, both with what they produce and with how they produce." *MECW* vol. 5, pp. 31–2.

37. Beyond a logical relation, the violence of class is an experience we undergo in selling our labor powers for a wage and working (or being unable to do so). And this experience is different depending on how one is raced, gendered, and so much else. But this is not quite the same as agreeing with Selma James that identity "is the very substance of class." Rather than "identity," which is itself still too abstract, the different lived experiences people actually have of being on the working side of the relational logic of class give class its substance. Rooting class in identity prompts James' conclusion that "The social power relations of the sexes, races, nations and generations are precisely, then, particularized forms of class relations," through which "one section of the class coloniz(es) another and through this capital impos(es) its own will on us all." In such a view the relation "class" was to name, and the specifically capitalist exploitation it was to make intelligible is lost. See James, "Sex, Race, and Class," in *Sex, Race and Class: The Perspective of Winning. A Selection of Writings 1952–2011* (Oakland: PM Press, 2012), pp. 92–101.

38. Derek Sayer, *Violence of Abstraction* (Oxford: Basil Blackwell, 1987), pp. 75–6.

39. Ibid., p. 77.

40. See David McNally and Sue Ferguson's interview with *Viewpoint Magazine*, "Social Reproduction Beyond Intersectionality," available at www.viewpointmag.com/2015/10/31/social-reproduction-beyond-intersectionality-an-interview-with-sue-ferguson-and-david-mcnally/.

41. Louise Thompson Patterson, "Toward a Brighter Dawn," *Woman Today*, 1936, available at www.viewpointmag.com/2015/10/31/toward-a-brighter-dawn-1936/.

42. Ashley Bohrer, Response to Barbara Foley's "Intersectionality: A Marxist Critique," *New Labor Forum*, first published online August 6, 2019.

43. Bohrer, "Intersectionality and Marxism," p. 69.

44. In response to David McNally and Sue Ferguson's suggestion that despite intersectionality's difficulties with causal-explanation, SRT can take intersectional insights on board, Bohrer writes, "McNally and Ferguson seem to suggest that the same categories, relations, and theories initially developed to respond to white, working-class, heterosexual, cisgender, able-bodied, women (social reproduction theory) can remain essentially unchanged, and respond productively, sensitively, and profoundly to the situation of people who fit none of these social locations." For Bohrer, their suggestion amounts to folding the rich legacy and varied goals of intersectionality into merely a moment of SRT. Bohrer, *Marxism and Intersectionality*, pp. 170–1, n. 19. Yet McNally and Ferguson acknowledge both "significant shortcomings of early social reproduction theory," and that "responding requires a lot of work, and a real commitment to learning from the best of anti-racist and anti-colonial theory and practice." McNally and Ferguson work in the spirit of improving SRT through its ties to lived history, especially the history of struggle. See McNally and Ferguson's "Social Reproduction Beyond Intersectionality." Bohrer herself develops SRT in this way in her "Wages for Immigration!

Labor and Social Reproduction Under Contemporary Capitalism," *Spectre* (Spring, 2020), pp. 48–61.

45. See Camfield, "Beyond Adding on Gender and Class."

46. See, for instance, Amanda Armstrong's excellent "Infrastructures of Injury," *Lies* 2, pp. 117–37, available at www.liesjournal.net/volume2.pdf.

47. None of this means that "class" as a relation of production is the *only* way to appreciate systemic oppressions. Even if Marx is right to hold that "the emancipation of the workers contains universal human emancipation—and it contains this, because the whole of human servitude is involved in the relation of the worker to production," it does not therefore follow, as Marx immediately claims, that "all relations of servitude are but modifications and consequences of this relation." "Estranged Labour," in *Economic and Philosophic Manuscripts of 1844* in *MECW* vol. 3, p. 280. There is a very significant difference between the claim that all forms of oppression ("the whole of human servitude") are "involved" in class as a relation of production, which SRT accepts, and the more reductive claim that all forms of oppression are nothing more than "modifications and consequences" of this relation.

48. This is why organizations developing resistance and struggle need to recognize and respond not only to the logic of class but also how racism, misogyny, transphobia, and other social determinations of class limit our liberatory horizons and capacities in ways that often reproduce the oppressive relations we are trying to abolish. See in particular the forceful call in Lorenzo Komboa Ervin's "The Progressive Plantation: Racism Inside White Radical Social Change Groups," available at https://libcom.org/files/plantation-for-libcom.pdf?fbclid=IwAR1OvGPOo6zdjLXbDfznve NZ8XQOzuDpEVfAWWFcFAP938nsdgtKdTtiv2k.

49. Marx, "On the Jewish Question," *MECW* vol. 3, p. 146.

50. Ibid., p. 149.

CHAPTER 6: THE SOCIALIST HORIZON OF EMANCIPATION

1. As quoted in Eric Blanc, *Red State Revolt: The Teacher's Strike Wave and Working Class Politics* (London: Verso, 2019), p. 24.

2. Heleodora was interviewed by International Women's Strike, New York City. Her full interview is available at https://publicseminar.org/2018/03/heleodora-street-vendors-project/.

3. Women make up 77 percent of US teachers, but only 52 percent are principals. See www.edweek.org/ew/articles/2016/11/16/few-women-run-the-nations-school-districts.html. Only 13.2 percent are superintendents. See www.aasa.org/SchoolAdministratorArticle.aspx?id=14492.

4. See p. 7 of "The State of Racial Diversity in the Educator Workforce," available at www2.ed.gov/rschstat/eval/highered/racial-diversity/state-racial-diversity-workforce.pdf.

5. https://nces.ed.gov/programs/coe/pdf/coe_cgc.pdf. I am making the assumption that there is great overlap between the socially recognized race

of parents and children, although of course this is not universally true and indeed today cannot be safely assumed in most cases of adoptive parenting.

6. See James Collins, "Social Reproduction in Classrooms and Schools," *Annual Review of Anthropology* 38:1, p. 33–48.

7. See Rosemary Hennessy, *Fires on the Border: The Passionate Politics of Labour Organising on the Mexican Frontera* (Minneapolis: University of Minnesota, 2013), pp. 125 ff.

8. As, for instance, was the case with how the patriarchal organization of household production found in tributary economies reorganized into so many species of contemporary misogyny.

9. This is precisely what Aimé Césaire criticized with the term "abstract Communists" in the interview with René Depestre included in *Discourse on Colonialsm*, trans. Joan Pinkham (New York: Monthly Review Press, 2000), pp. 79–94, p. 85.

10. Marx and Engels, *Communist Manifesto*, *MECW* vol. 6, p. 515.

11. Ibid., p. 519.

12. The Street Vendor Project does precisely this by organizing vendors to fight for expanded legal recognition and protection.

13. Marx, "On the Jewish Question," *MECW* vol. 3, p. 153.

14. Ibid., p. 155.

15. See, for instance, Marta Russell, "What Disability Civil Rights Cannot Do," *Disability & Society*, 17:2 (2002), pp. 117–35, and Alan Sears "Situating Sexuality in Social Reproduction," *Historical Materialism* 24:2 (2016), pp. 138–63, especially pp. 138–40, p. 159.

16. I appreciate "horizon" as a framing device for two further reasons. First, it suggests we can see both the division between and points of connection where our ground meets the air—where our embodied practical activities differ from but are in constant relation to ideas and ideologies. Second, the planar form of a "horizon" suggests the levelling, democratic, and broadly anti-hierarchical or anti-authoritarian conditions of freedom. I think it is important to hold onto this metaphor as a way to situate freedom. It makes the free development and direction of our need-satisfying powers a structuring possibility of our world, here and now. At the level of ideas and what we aim for the horizon is both present as a possibility and provides a point of orientation for the development of struggle. Jodi Dean has developed this idea in *The Communist Horizon* (London: Verso, London, 2012).

17. See Peter Hudis, *Marx's Concept of the Alternative to Capitalism* (Chicago: Haymarket, 2013). William Clare Roberts develops this line of thinking in "Marx's Social Republic: Political not Metaphysical," *Historical Materialism* 27:2 (2019), pp. 41–58. The "horizon" as multiple, and opening possibilities for non-capitalist social reproduction is explored in "Crisis in the Class Relation," *Endnotes* 2, available at https://endnotes.org.uk/issues/2/en/endnotes-crisis-in-the-class-relation.

18. The Combahee River Collective's "A Black Feminist Perspective," for instance, adopts this view, and includes imperialism and presumptions of heterosexuality in its critical sights as well.

19. Sara Farris' analysis of "femonationalist" projects shows how in the name of civic integration and freedom from domestic tyranny, immigrant women to the EU are shunted into disempowering forms of socially reproductive labor that produce more freedom for EU citizen women. See, in particular, chapter four of her *In the Name of Women's Rights: The Rise of Femonationalism* (Durham: Duke University Press, 2017).

20. See Street Vendors Project's legal director Matthew Shapiro's analysis of "Broken Windows" and "Quality of Life" policing in www.eater. com/2019/11/19/20971122/subway-food-vendor-crackdown-nyc-mta-sf-bart.

21. See, for instance, Eve L. Ewing's *Ghosts in the Schoolyard: Racism and School Closings on Chicago's South Side* (Chicago: University of Chicago Press, 2018).

22. Bhaskar Sunkara, *The Socialist Manifesto: The Case for Radical Politics in an Era of Extreme Inequality* (New York: Basic Books, 2019), p. 26.

23. Ibid., pp. 26–7.

24. Marx, *Capital* vol. 1, *MECW* vol. 35, p. 89.

CHAPTER 7: SOCIAL REPRODUCTION THEORY
AND POLITICAL STRATEGY

1. "Chicago Teachers Are Threatening to Strike Against New Mayor Lori Lightfoot. Here's Why," available at www.salon.com/2019/08/11/chicago-teachers-are-threatening-to-strike-against-new-mayor-lori-lightfoot-heres-why_partner.

2. As quoted in Blanc, *Red State Revolt*, p. 71.

3. Marx, "Contribution to a Critique of Hegel's Philosophy of Law: Introduction," *MECW* vol. 3, p. 182.

4. I am grateful to Hagen List, who suggested proximity to the body as an organizing theme for the gendered nature of women's socially reproductive work, and to Michelle O'Brien for helping me think through the family resemblance across different kinds of socially reproductive work that women tend to do.

5. See "The Impossibility of the Women's Strike Is Exactly Why It's So Necessary," available at https://novaramedia.com/2017/03/06/the-impossibility-of-the-international-womens-strike-is-exactly-why-its-so-necessary/.

6. See, for instance, Cinzia Arruzza, Tithi Bhattacharya, and Nancy Fraser, *Feminism for the 99%: A Manifesto* (London: Verso, 2019), pp. 6 ff.

7. There are, of course, those who prefer sex work to other equally available options, as well as those who are coerced into sex work by forces beyond gender oppression. Depending on the context, sex work can therefore be a deeply violent form of disempowerment, a way of scraping together a living, or a freer form of developing and actualizing one's capacities. Still, excluding sex workers from a political vision of emancipation, either by morally

condemning it or by presuming all sex workers are equally free to choose other lines of work, would amount to further entrenching trans people's (in particular Latina and Black trans women's) oppressions.

8. See http://links.org.au/international-womens-strike-platform. Kate Doyle Griffiths, Michelle O'Brien, Cinzia Arruzza, Tithi Bhattacharya, Magally Miranda, Susana Draper, and myself, all theorists of social reproduction, were active in the US organization of International Women's Strike. I have benefitted tremendously from informal conversations with each of them, from listening to and reading their work, and especially from our shared work of organizing together.

9. In "The Logic of Gender" in *Endnotes* the writers take a similar stance on the denaturalization of gender, but are less optimistic. For them the social evolution of capital itself denaturalizes gender. But there is little on how social agents with some powers to gender-otherwise participate in this process. Likewise, for Roswitha Scholz "value dissociation" produces gender in historically varying and never entirely subsumed feminine ways. But her goal is to theorize gender through value-theoretic ends and therefore at a degree of abstraction far removed from the particulars of agency. See Scholz, "Patriarchy and Commodity Society: Gender Without the Body," *Mediations* 27, pp. 1–2, available at www.mediationsjournal.org/articles/patriarchy-and-commodity-society.

10. I am paraphrasing Marx who makes this point about history more generally in "The Eighteenth Brumaire of Louis Napoleon": "Men make their own history, but they do not make it just as they please; they do not make it under circumstances chosen by themselves, but under circumstances directly encountered, given and transmitted from the past. The tradition of all the dead generations weighs like a nightmare on the brain of the living." *MECW* vol. 11, p. 99. This "sedimented weight" codes some activities as masculine even when women do them, and vice versa. See Judith Halberstam, *Feminine Masculinity* (Durham: Duke University Press, 1998), especially pp. 57 ff. Peter Drucker shows, in a class-sensitive way, how neoliberal capitalist conditions determine the scope for sex and gender freedom. See Peter Drucker, *Warped: Gay Normality and Queer Anticapitalism* (Chicago: Haymarket, 2015).

11. Following Butler we do this through iterative practices or "performances" of our gender, but also, following Kevin Floyd, these include the constrained patterns of consuming subjects deeply influenced by "disciplinary social consumption," p. 35 of *The Reification of Desire* (Minneapolis: University of Minnesota Press, 2009). As Cinzia Arruzza has argued, our genders temporally unfold not only in consumption, but in the sphere of circulation as well. See, Arruzza, "Gender as Social Temporality: Butler (and Marx)," *Historical Materialism* 23: 1, pp. 28–52. Yet I think it is important to also conceive of gender through our powers for social and self-*reproduction*. See, for instance, Amy De'Ath's passing use of Elson in "Gender and Social Reproduction," p. 1544. For Maya Gonzalez, gender is tied to the indirect, unwaged market mediations through which labor powers are produced

and reproduced. See "The Gendered Circuit: The Arcane of Reproduction," *Viewpoint Magazine*, available at www.viewpointmag.com/2013/09/28/ the-gendered-circuit-reading-the-arcane-of-reproduction/.

12. Frigga Haug, in *Beyond Female Masochism* (London: Verso, 1992), provides insightful commentary on how women's chosen forms of resistance against oppressive working conditions, both in the home and beyond it, form a crucial part of women's evolving relations to the "feminine" and "feminization." See in particular pp. 127–9.

13. See Kate Doyle Griffith, "The Only Way Out Is Through," available at www.versobooks.com/blogs/3709-the-only-way-out-is-through-a-reply-to-melinda-cooper. There is, of course, not a single form of queer social reproduction, as working class queer people are as diverse in needs and powers as the straight population. See the Gender Studies master's thesis by Siân F. Bradley, "Queer Work: Productivity, Reproduction and Change" (Linköping University, 2016), pp. 40–50.

14. See Gleeson, "Transition and Abolition" and "An Aviary of Queer Social Reproduction."

15. Some do both, as was the case with the STAR (Street Transvestite Action Revolutionaries) organization, which developed housing for queer youth as part of its broader revolutionary goals.

16. Sears, "Situating Sexuality," p. 160.

17. Jones' "An End to the Neglect of the Problems of the Negro Woman!" for instance, charts Black women's centrality and evolving contributions to Black social reproduction.

18. See Michelle Esther O'Brien, "Why Queer Workers Make Good Organisers" forthcoming in *Work, Employment and Society*.

19. See Mariarosa Dalla Costa, "Capitalism and Reproduction," in *Women and the Subversion of the Community: A Mariarosa Dalla Costa Reader*, ed. Camille Barbagallo (Oakland: PM Press, 2019), pp. 217–28, p. 225.

20. See Ferguson, *Women and Work*, pp. 130–7 for a strong argument to move SRT's political commitments towards challenging capital's violence, not merely finding alternative modes of surviving within it.

21. See Kate Doyle Griffiths, "Labor Valorization and Social Reproduction— What Is Valuable about the Labor Theory of Value?" in *Comparative Literature and Culture* 22:2 (2020).

22. Sarah Jaffe, "How Chicago Teachers Built Power between Strikes," October 22, 2019, available at https://progressive.org/dispatches/chicago-teachers-built-power-between-strikes-jaffe-191022/.

23. To be sure, the strike was also to improve teachers' working conditions. Charles Post shows teachers' unions' struggle for better social conditions, in particular the fight against racism, needs to be grounded in the bread and butter issues central to the job itself. "Social Unionism Without the Workplace?" *New Politics*, Winter, 2013, available at https://newpol.org/review/social-unionism-without-workplace/.

24. See Rebecca Burns, "Chicago's Citywide Strike Just Spread to Charter Schools," October 23, 2019, available at http://inthesetimes.com/working/

entry/22133/chicago-teachers-union-passages-charter-school-strike-seiu. The charter school teachers were demanding not only wage increases, but safety from Immigration and Customs Enforcement (ICE) more nurses, resources for special-education students and English language learners, and counselors and social workers to help students who are refugees cope with their trauma.

POSTSCRIPT: SOCIAL REPRODUCTION THEORY IN AND BEYOND THE PANDEMIC

1. For instance, Mike Davis, *The Monster at Our Door: The Global Threat of Avian Flu* (New York: New Press, 2005), Rob Wallace, *Big Farms Make Big Flu: Dispatches on Influenza, Agribusiness, and the Nature of Science* (New York: Monthly Review Press, 2016), and David Quammen, *Spillover: Animal Infections and the Next Human Pandemic* (New York: W.W. Norton, 2012).

Index

Thanks to our Patreon Subscribers:

Abdul Alkalimat
Andrew Perry

Who have shown their generosity and comradeship in difficult times.

Check out the other perks you get by subscribing to our Patreon – visit patreon.com/plutopress.

Subscriptions start from £3 a month.

The Pluto Press Newsletter

Hello friend of Pluto!

Want to stay on top of the best radical books we publish?

Then sign up to be the first to hear about our new books, as well as special events, podcasts and videos.

You'll also get 50% off your first order with us when you sign up.

Come and join us!

Go to bit.ly/PlutoNewsletter